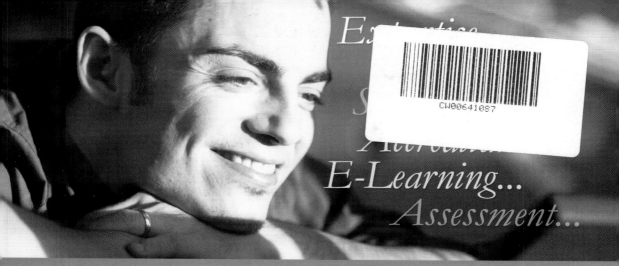

*Expertise*

*S...*

*Accreditation*

*E-Learning...*

*Assessment...*

# Word, Excel, Access, PowerPoint...
# DO YOU HAVE WHAT IT TAKES?

*Test yourself FREE:*

# www.moustest.com
**and prepare for your MOUS accreditation.**

*Train on line:*

# www.123training.com
**and build your skills.**

# Getting started
## with your computer
### and the Windows XP environment

# ENI Publishing LTD

5 D Hillgate Place
18-20 Balham Hill
London SW12 9ER

Tel: 020 8673 3366
Fax: 020 8673 2277

e-mail: publishing@ediENI.com
http://www.eni-publishing.com

English edition by Andrew BLACKBURN
**WAY IN** collection directed by Corinne Hervo

## Foreword

This book has been written for beginners who want to know how to get the most from their PC using Windows XP and the different features that their Windows applications offer.

You can consult the different parts of this book separately but they have been designed to be taken in order. This way, you will first discover the different hardware components of your computer and how they fit together. When you have connected everything up, the second part of this book will show you how to start your computer and work comfortably in the Windows environment. The third part deals with three applications that many computers offer: the Word word processor, and the Works integrated software package. You can use these applications to create documents and save them on your hard disk, while the fourth part describes how you can use the Windows Explorer to manage your documents. If you have an Internet connection you can take your first trip on this "information highway" using the fifth part of this book as your guide. The sixth part describes typical problems you may encounter together with the messages that will appear on your screen in such situations: this final part will prepare you to deal with such problems, if and when they occur.

This book is not just for reading; it is essentially to be put into practice. Sit down at your computer and try out the actions described by following the examples. Keep this book close to your computer and you will find it a useful reference for finding a function or term that you may have forgotten.

Not only will you find information on the features that Windows offers, you will also find tips on what not to do and what not to forget, as well as convenient shortcuts to help you save time. You can often carry out the same action using the mouse, the keyboard or the menus. These symbols will help you between each type of method:  for a keyboard method,  for a method that uses the mouse and  for the method using the menus. You may also come across the following symbols:

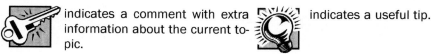 indicates a comment with extra information about the current topic. indicates a useful tip.

**The only way to learn about your computer is to use it: settle down in front of your screen, prop this book up next to the keyboard... and you will soon see that your computer is not as complicated as you might have thought.**

# Table
## of contents

# Table
## of contents

# Table
## of contents

# Table
## of contents

**Works: a software suite** Chapter 3.2

Starting Microsoft Works                                            80

Using the Task Launcher                                             82

Creating a document                                                 84

Description of the spreadsheet window                               85

Moving around a spreadsheet                                         86

Entering data                                                       87

Editing the contents of a cell                                      88

Deleting the contents of a cell                                     89

Entering a calculation formula                                      89

Inserting a function into a formula                                 90

Copying the contents of a cell to adjacent cells                    91

Inserting rows/columns                                              92

Deleting rows/columns                                               93

Changing column widths                                              93

Changing row heights                                                94

Formatting characters                                               95

Saving, opening and closing a Works document                        97

Using the print preview                                             97

Printing a document                                                 98

Closing Works applications                                          100

# Table
## of contents

# Table
## of contents

# Table
## of contents

## Introduction

Computing is becoming increasingly important for all of us, young or old. In fact, computers are involved in some form in practically everything we do today and who can guess what computing's role might be tomorrow?

Charles Babbage designed the first general purpose computer in England in 1833. This so-called Analytical Engine followed instructions from punched cards. In the next century, electronics were used to dramatic effect. An early example of an electronic computer was the ENIAC. Built in the United States in 1946 out of 17,468 electronic vacuum tubes, the ENIAC weighed 30 tonnes and covered 72 square metres!

The miniaturisation of electronic components led to a veritable revolution in the computing world. A key event in this progression was the invention of the microprocessor by Intel in 1971: in comparison to the ENIAC, the Intel 4004 weighed a few grams, was 4.2 cm long and 3.2 cm wide! Since that date, the microprocessor, the central computing element, has undergone numerous developments leading to the rapid expansion of computing in the 1980's.

During this period, two great computing hardware families came to the fore: Apple and IBM.

The Apple computer, later to become the Macintosh, was the only one to offer a graphical environment with icons and the use of a mouse: this was the first version of the interface that all micro-computers provide today. Today, graphics and multimedia professionals frequently use Apple equipment.

For their part, IBM launched a new type of computing hardware, called the PC or Personal Computer. Up until this time, only large industries used computing, in the form of computers wired up to huge "cabinets" that stored all the information. The PC offered computing for all: used at first in the workplace, the PC later came into the home. Several companies, in particular, Microsoft, developed this new market, offering IBM-compatible PCs.

Micro-computers at that time used 8086 microprocessors and ran in the MS-DOS interface: this consisted of a black screen on which you wrote specific words and phrases, similar to those of a programming language.

From this time, processing capacity on average has doubled every year. The 8086 gave way to the 286 (with over three times as much processing power) which in turn was superseded by the 386 and then by the 486 (which was four times faster than the 386). Several versions of this processor appeared, with higher and higher processing speeds, which are measured in MHz: the first 486 ran at 25 MHz, while the final 486 processed at 100 MHz. In 1993, Intel brought out a new processor, called the Pentium, which was able to transmit data twice as fast as any of its predecessors. Intel has since brought out the Pentium 2, Pentium 3, Celeron and Pentium 4 processors.

# Introduction

In parallel with these hardware developments, the software has been changing too. The text-mode environment on MS-DOS gave way to the graphical Windows environment: Windows has opened the floodgates to multimedia (sound, pictures and video) and to the Internet, transforming the computer into an indispensable and fascinating tool.

# 1st

## Part

You have just bought your first computer and you are impatient to get started with it. Before you can work with your machine, you need to plug all its different parts together! This first part will explain what all the pieces of your computer do and how to connect them to each other.

# Connecting up your computer

*Hardware changes so fast these days that you can expect your computer to remain up-to-date for only about three months (although you would naturally expect it to work much longer!). Since they first appeared, the micro-computer's external appearance has altered relatively little. On the other hand, its internal capabilities have changed beyond recognition.*

## A TYPICAL COMPUTER

main unit

screen (or monitor)

mouse

keyboard

The example computer above provides only the essential items you need to use it. As this chapter will describe in the following pages, you can add many devices to this basic configuration (such as a printer, a scanner, a joystick and so forth).

*The main unit is the heart of the micro-computer. All the other micro-computer items are connected to this cabinet.*

## MAIN UNIT

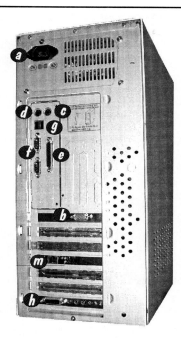

▓ The back panel of the main unit provides a number of sockets (or **ports**):

- the **power socket** (a) connects your computer to the mains power supply.
- the **video port** (b) connects your screen to the main unit.
- the **PS/2 ports** (c and d) connect your mouse and keyboard to the main unit. You can use the connector colours to help you: generally green for the mouse and purple for the keyboard.
- the **parallel port** (e) allows you to connect a number of different items (called devices), such as a printer, for example.
- **serial ports** (f) are used to connect other devices such as a modem or a mouse.
- **USB ports** (g) as with parallel or serial ports, are for connecting devices, such as a scanner. Devices that are compatible with this type of port bear the following symbol: **USB** *UNIVERSAL SERIAL BUS* .

- the **modem port** (m) allows you to connect to a telephone plug.
- the **sound card** (h) allows you to connect loudspeakers or a headset (i), a microphone (k), a hi-fi system (j) to record to your hard disk from an audio CD or cassette and a joystick (l) to play video games.

The following symbols denote these different connectors:

     (i) loudspeakers or headphones (generally light green)

     (j) hi-fi equipment (generally light blue)

     (k) microphone (can be pink)

     (l) joystick

 Some main units can relay the mains power supply to the screen. If present, this connection is below connection (a) and has a similar form except that it is a female socket. According to the main unit concerned, these connections may be arranged differently. The ends of the mains cable that you

must connect to these sockets look like this: 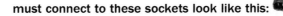.

*The other large item of your computer is, of course, the screen. The screen displays all the information that you enter and data that the computer transmits.*

## SCREEN

※ The screen takes two different cables:

- the mains cable (a) that powers the screen; this cable is identical to the power cable of the main unit.
- the video cable (b) that connects the screen to the video port of the main unit.

**You may be able to connect the screen to the mains power supply via the main unit (as indicated on page 14).**

The screen is the heaviest element of your computer and you may have some difficulty getting it out of its packaging. Perhaps the most convenient method is to open the top of the box then, holding the top flaps aside, carefully turn it upside down on the floor and simply lift the cardboard box off its contents: the polystyrene packaging should continue to hold the screen in place.

# Connecting up your computer

*The two main devices for entering information and instructions are the keyboard and the mouse: you use the keyboard to enter text and the mouse to open menus, choose options and so forth.*

## KEYBOARD AND MOUSE

※ You connect the keyboard to port (c) and the mouse to port (d) on the main unit (see p. 13).

Most computers indicate what you should connect to ports (c) and (d) by a small drawing above or below each of these ports (symbolizing a keyboard or a mouse).

 You can use other devices to transmit information to your computer, such as a barcode reader or a headset with vocal software.

Nowadays, new types of keyboard and mouse are available that transmit data by radio. This type of equipment does not need cables running across your desk and gives more freedom in using your keyboard and mouse. These devices are battery driven and come with transceivers that connect to the corresponding ports (to port (c) for a keyboard and port (d) for a mouse).

Getting to know the hardware

To accommodate multimedia applications, most computers provide a sound card and loudspeakers so that you can listen to audio CDs or multimedia programs (on CD-ROM or the Internet) with accompanying sound.

## LOUDSPEAKERS

 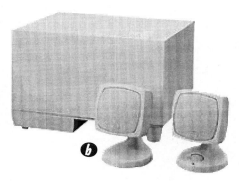

- ⬚ Connect the loudspeaker plug to the connection (i) on the sound card (cf. p. 14).

- ⬚ In general, only one of the loudspeakers provides controls to switch them on and off and to control their volume, balance and possibly their tone.

- ⬚ There are several types of loudspeaker: you may have ordinary speakers (a) or subwoofers and satellites (b). Computer subwoofers and satellites offer sound quality comparable to that of hi-fi equipment.

 Some loudspeakers connect to the mains power supply via the main unit. In this case, you connect the speaker power cable between the main unit power socket (see (a) on page 13) and the screen power socket.

# How your computer works

*When you have connected up your computer, it is ready to go. Before you start using it, here is an overview of your computer hardware to explain how each part of your computer works.*

## MAIN UNIT

The main unit is the central part of the computer, as it receives and stores all the information (or data) that you enter.

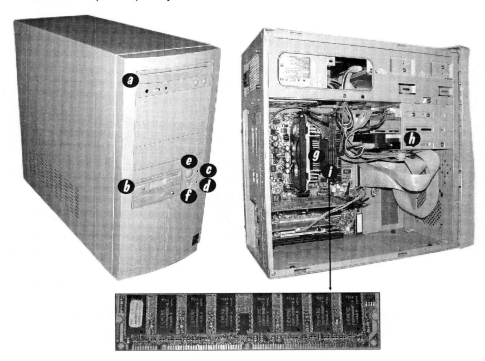

- The front of your main unit presents the following items:
  - a **DVD-ROM drive** (a) can play CDs as well as DVDs. It works in the same way as a CD drive on a hi-fi system. The DVD-ROM is a multimedia storage unit device that can contain text, image, graphic, animation and video data: it can contain a complete encyclopaedia, for example, or a complete movie. Some computers offer only a **CD-ROM drive**: a CD-ROM is exactly the same size as a DVD-ROM, but it cannot store as much information (for example, a CD-ROM could contain only about 10 seconds of a film!).

- a **floppy drive** (b) works with 3½ inch square "floppy" disks that are generally marked HD (High Density). You can write (save) information onto these disks. Floppy disks provide a supplement to the hard disk and allow you to "transport" the information they contain more easily. Floppy disks usually offer a capacity of 1.44 MB (one million bytes is roughly equivalent to one million characters).
- the **power indicator** (c) shows as a green light when the central unit is switched on.
- the **hard disk indicator** (d) shows as a red/orange light when the hard disk is working (when you ask for information from the hard disk or save your data to the hard disk, for example).
- the **power button** (e) allows you to switch your main unit on or off.

Your main unit also contains the following items inside:

- the **microprocessor** (g) is the heart and brain of your computer. It knows where every piece of information is and can run millions or even billions of instructions per second. A clock is associated with the microprocessor that indicates how fast it runs in MHz (MegaHertz). Modern microprocessors run at between 1000 MHz and 2.2 GHz (GigaHertz).
- the **hard disk** (h) contains the information your computer needs to run properly and can store the data you want to keep (save). The capacity of modern hard disks is measured in GB (GigaBytes, which correspond to billions of characters), while the capacity of older hard disks is expressed in MB (MegaBytes, which correspond to millions of characters). Today's hard disks generally have capacities from 6 to 80 GB, although certain professionals use computers with hard disks of 2 TB (2 TeraBytes or 2000 GigaBytes).
- **SDRAM memory** (i) stores data before it is saved to the hard disk. This memory is cleared when your computer powers down. The capacity of this memory is generally expressed in MB (MegaBytes). It comes in sticks of capacity expressed in MB. You can increase your RAM memory capacity simply by adding extra sticks. Nowadays, RAM capacities vary from 128 MB to 3 GB. The higher this capacity is, the quicker and more easily the microprocessor will be able to handle large quantities of data.
- You can add boards into any empty slots (for example, you may want to add a board to connect a joystick). The number of slots will depend on the size of the main unit.

# How your computer works

- It is important to have a clear idea of what you want to do with your computer, before you decide what capacity (or speed) you need for each of these components (this is called configuring your computer). For example, for office needs (involving word processor or spreadsheet applications, such as those that this book describes) a 600 MHz microprocessor with a 15 GB hard disk and 128 MB of SDRAM should be sufficient. On the other hand, if you want to run video games on your computer you will need a higher grade configuration. As a final example, if you want to process images, you are likely to need a 1.8 GHz microprocessor with a 40 GB hard disk and 512 MB of SDRAM.

 Some main units provide another button next to the power button that is much smaller, much more discrete and generally red in colour. This is the Reset button (f). You can use this button to restart your computer, as a last resort when you have a problem.

Some main units provide an extra on/off button on the back panel.

*The screen displays information. You can adjust it for visual comfort at any time.*

## SCREEN

- To switch your screen on, use the power button (a).

You can use the other buttons (h) to adjust the image size and position along with the brightness and contrast, as on a television:

- button (b) enlarges or reduces the image, horizontally.
- button (c) enlarges or reduces the image, vertically.
- button (d) moves the image to the right and to the left: you can use this button to centre the image horizontally on the screen.
- button (e) moves the image up and down: you can use this button to centre the image vertically on the screen.

Increasingly, screens provide on-screen menus that appear on the screen when you press the **Menu** button.

**Other screens provide these buttons behind a panel that you press to open at the bottom of the screen.**

Most modern screens are designed to reduce visual fatigue. However, you may still want to add an external filter on your screen.

*Above all, a computer is a machine to which you give instructions (by opening a menu and applying a colour to a text, for example) and into which you enter data (such as the text of your letter or the name you want to give to the file that contains it). You send this data to your computer via your keyboard. Computer keyboards have changed a lot from the typewriter keyboards on which they were originally based. A computer keyboard offers several sets of keys.*

## KEYBOARD

- The "typewriter" (or alphanumerical) keyboard (A) provides keys for entering characters (letters and numbers); some of these keys offer specific features.

- The **Caps Lock** key (a) locks the keyboard into uppercase (capitals) mode; when you press this key the **Caps Lock** indicator (1) lights up. If you press a letter key, your letter will appear in uppercase.
- To cancel the Caps Lock, press the **Caps Lock** key (a) again; this time the **Caps Lock** indicator (1) goes off. If you press a letter key, your letter will appear in lowercase (see the note at the end of this section).

- You do not need to lock your keyboard into uppercase mode if you want to make only the first letter of a word a capital: in this case, it is simpler to press the **Shift** key ⬆ (b) and keeping it pressed down, press the key of the letter you want to appear in uppercase (then release the letter key followed by the **Shift** key). If you press the **Shift** key ⬆ (b) and keep it pressed down while you press the %⃟ key, the % sign will appear on the screen.

- You can use the **Tab** key (c) to place a word or a text at a position that you have defined beforehand by setting a tab stop (cf. Word: a word processor - Inserting a tab).
  You can also use this key to go in turn to each of the different options of a dialog box.

- You can use the **Backspace** key (d) to delete the latest characters you entered.

- The **Enter** key (e) is fundamental to using your computer, as you can press it to confirm information that you want to send to your computer. You will also use it often when you enter text, to go on to the next line.

▨ The alphanumerical keyboard (A) also offers a number of specific keys:

- You can use the **Control** (f) and **Alt** (g) keys together with other keys and with the mouse: the result will depend on the application you are using at the time.

- You can use the **Alt Gr** key (h) to enter the third character that some keys show: For example, to enter the € (Euro) symbol, hold down the Alt Gr key while you press the €⃟ key.

- Use the **spacebar** (k) to insert a space in your text (between two words, for example).

- Use the **Windows** key (i) to open the Windows start menu.

- You can use the **Menu** key (j) to open the menu associated with the item that is currently active (this is called the shortcut menu).

▨ Each of the **function keys** (B) can provide a different action that, in general, will depend on the application concerned. In all applications, however, the **F1** key opens the help window for the application you are currently using.

**Getting to know the hardware**

- You can use the two navigation key areas (C) and (D), shown below, to go to the different items you see on the screen.

When you enter information, you must let the computer know where you want it to include this information. For example, suppose that you are editing a text and you want to add in some new text; you must start by going to the paragraph where you want your new text to appear. Different applications represent this position in different ways: a text application, for example, will indicate this position by a blinking vertical line, called an **insertion point**. Use the arrow keys to move the insertion point around in the text:

- upwards (k): in a text, press this key once to go to the line above.
- downwards (l): in a text, press this key once to go to the line below.
- to the left (m): in a text, press this key once to move the insertion point before the previous character.
- to the right (n): in a text, press this key once to move the insertion point before the next character.

The upper navigation pad (c) offers four keys that allow you to move further quickly and two keys with editing features:

- Press the **PgUp** key (o) in a text to go to the previous page.
- Press the **PgDn** key (p) in a text to go to the next page.
- Press the **Home** key (q) in a text to go to the beginning of the current line.
- Press the **End** key (r) in a text to go to the end of the current line.

- Use the **Insert** key (s) to activate overtype mode; press again to return to insert mode. With insert mode active, the characters you enter appear between the characters already in the text. With overtype mode active, the characters you enter replace existing characters.
- Use the **Delete** key (t) in a text to delete characters to the right of the insertion point.

Here is the numeric keypad or number pad (E):

- The **Num Lock** key activates and deactivates the number lock. When the number lock is active, the **Num Lock** indicator (2) is lit (the number lock is active, by default): in this mode, when you press a number pad key labelled with a number and an arrow, for example, the number will appear on the screen. On the other hand, when you deactivate the **Num Lock**, the keys act like the corresponding keys on the navigation areas (arrows, **PgUp**, **PgDn** and so forth).
- The number pad provides mathematical operator keys (+ to add, - to subtract, * to multiply and / to divide).
- It also contains an **Enter** key, which acts in the same way as the **Enter** key in the alphanumeric area (this is convenient to use when you are entering numbers).

In addition to the keys described above, the keyboard offers the following keys (F):

- the **Print Screen** (Prt Sc) key saves an image of the screen as it currently appears, so that you can print it.

- the **Scroll Lock** key locks and unlocks the cursor, relative to the arrow keys: if an application supports this key, your cursor (insertion point) will stay in the same position even if you scroll the page. When the scroll lock is on, the **Scroll Lock** indicator (3) lights up. Modern computing applications support this key less and less.
- the **Pause** key stops and restarts the flow of information on the screen, provided that the current application supports it. As with the **Scroll Lock** key, this feature is becoming obsolete.
- the **Esc** key is situated in the top left corner of the keyboard. In certain cases, you can use this key to cancel any text you have just entered or to cancel a web page download you have requested.

 On some keyboards, you must press the **Shift** key to cancel the **Caps Lock**.

*The mouse has become practically indispensable in the Windows environment. Although you may find this tool difficult to use at first, you will soon work with it quite naturally.*

## MOUSE

- You can use the mouse with certain screen items (for example, to open a menu and select an option). The current screen position of the mouse often appears as a white arrow called a **pointer** (or sometimes a **cursor**). Slide the mouse on your mouse pad to move the pointer to the required item (with most mice, the movements of the screen pointer corresponds to the rolling of a hard rubber ball that protrudes from the under surface of the mouse).
- When you have reached the required screen item, carry out most actions (such as opening a menu, for example) by pressing the left button of the mouse then releasing it. This is called clicking.
- To carry out some actions you must double-click your mouse: this means that you must press the button then release it, twice in quick succession.

- To select several screen items, you may want to drag over them with your mouse. Dragging involves pressing the left mouse button and holding this button down while sliding the mouse then releasing the mouse button when you are happy with the result. For example, you can drag your mouse over several items so as to select all of them; when you are happy with your selection, release the mouse button.

- Clicking the right-hand mouse button is called right-clicking. You can right-click a screen item to open its shortcut menu. The shortcut menu provides options that are specific to the item concerned (this is the item that is under your mouse pointer when you click).

- The modern mouse often provides a scroll wheel between the left and right buttons. You can use this wheel to scroll through a document (instead of using the navigation keys, such as [PgUp] and [PgDn], for example).

**Some mice provide three buttons. You can set up your mouse so that it will carry out a specific task when you press its middle button.**

You must clean your mouse regularly. Remove the rubber ball underneath the mouse and scrape the rollers that run against this ball with an instrument that will not scratch them (your nails, for example) so as to remove the debris that tends to adhere to them.

# Other external devices

*A device, or peripheral device, is any part of your computer that is not the CPU (Central Processing Unit) or the computer working memory. An external device is a device that is outside your main unit, such as your mouse or your keyboard. This section will describe some other external devices you can connect to your computer system. There are many different types of external device for varying needs, such as a printer to print your documents on paper, a modem to connect to the Internet, a CD-R drive or CD burner, a ZIP drive to backup your data, a scanner to enter your photos into your computer in the form of digital files, a digital camera, a joystick and so forth.*

## PRINTERS

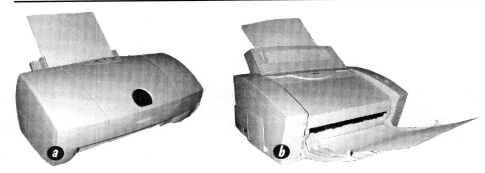

- Two types of printer are commonly used today: ink jet printers (a) and laser printers (b). Laser printers usually print black and white, as colour laser printers are quite expensive (approximately £ 1400 (€ 2 300), as opposed to £ 200 to £ 240 (€ 300 to 400) for a black and white model). Laser printers use toner cartridges (as with photocopy machines) and/or drums, according to the model and the make. Ink jet printers usually print colour and black and white. They use ink cartridges and most general purpose models are available in a price range from £ 50 to £ 130 (€ 75 to 220).

- A printer is supplied with:
  - toner or ink cartridges: you must change these regularly, which contributes to your running costs. The price of these consumable items varies according to the manufacturer.
  - a mains power cable (220 V).
  - a printer driver: a CD-ROM generally contains this item, which allows the operating system to recognise the printer. When you have connected up the printer you must install the printer software using this CD-ROM (cf. Managing folders and files - Installing a printer).

The printer cable is generally not supplied with the printer. This cable links the printer to the computer main unit and carries information (data) between them. According to the type of printer cable you use, you connect the (c) end of this cable to the computer's parallel port (cf. Main unit) and the (d) end of this cable to the printer or the (e) end of the cable to the computer's USB port (cf. Main unit) and the (f) end of the cable to the printer.

**Not all ink jet printers use the same type of colour cartridges: some ink jet printers use one black and white cartridge and one cartridge for each of the basic colours, while other ink jet printers use one black and white cartridge and one cartridge for all the colours. With the first approach, you need replace only the colour cartridge that has run out. On the other hand, with the second approach, you must replace the complete, unique colour cartridge as soon as it runs out of one of its colours (the colour blue, for example).**

When equipped with special photo paper and cartridges, some ink jet printers offer a print quality similar to that of photos.

# Other external devices

*With the continuing craze for the Internet, you are probably eager to start surfing the Web. First, you must connect a modem between your main unit and your telephone socket.*

## MODEM

You can use a modem to send and receive data, such as messages and faxes, across the telephone network.

▓ There are two types of modem:

- An internal modem resides as a board in the main unit. This type of modem works only when the computer is switched on. It is supplied with a CD-ROM for installing the application that will allow you to use the modem. You can see its position on the back panel of your main unit by the presence of a telephone socket.

- An external modem is housed in a separate casing that you can connect to any micro-computer. Most external modems operate even when your computer is switched off. This means that it can receive messages and faxes even when your computer is switched off. You can connect an external modem to your main unit, generally via one of the two serial ports (f) or one of the USB ports (g) (see the main unit illustration on page 13).

▓ An external modem is supplied with:

- a telephone cable,
- a manual,

- a serial cable (a) or USB cable (b),

- a serial adapter, which allows you to add a serial connection, when both of your serial ports are already in use.

*Increasingly, computer manufacturers provide the CD-R drive as standard equipment. You can use a CD-R drive (also called a CD writer or burner) to make copies of your audio or data CD-ROMs and to archive your personal data.*

## CD-R DRIVE

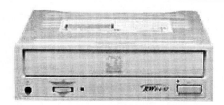

▓ A CD-R drive is a CD player onto which you can also copy information. You copy this information onto a special CD, which can be of two types: CDR (CD-Recordable) and CDRW (CD-Rewritable). You can write to a CDR only once, whereas you can write to CDRWs more than once.

▓ Even if your computer was not supplied with a CD-R drive, you can still add one. A CD-R drive looks like a normal CD drive and, as with a normal CD drive, you install it in the upper part of the main unit. The CD-R comes with:

- a manual,
- an installation CD-ROM containing an application that allows your computer to recognise it (a driver) and an application for copying CDs.

# Other external devices

Important note: generally speaking, you are authorized to copy a CD for your personal use, provided that you own the original. However, it is illegal to use such copies for commercial purposes.

DVD-R drives (or DVD burners) are also available that allow you to copy DVDs. When you produce DVD-Rs in this way, you can play them on both DVD drives and DVD video players. At the time of going to press, the capacity of DVD-Rs was limited to approximately 10 GB (4.7 GB per side).

*One of the golden rules of computing is to make at least one and possibly two backup copies of your important data. In this way, you can still work with your backup copy, even if you can no longer open a file (either because you overwrote or deleted it by accident) or for technical reasons (if the system can no longer find the file on your hard disk, for example). You can create backup copies in several ways. One of the simplest ways is to write your data to a ZIP disk.*

## ZIP DRIVE

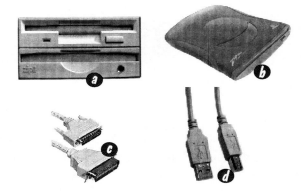

▪ As with a floppy drive, the ZIP drive writes data to a removable storage medium. The main difference between these two types of disk is the capacity. The capacity of a floppy disk is only 1.44 MB (approximately one million characters, for example). On the other hand, on a ZIP disk, you can store 100 MB (approximately equivalent to 70 floppy disks) or 250 MB (approximately equivalent to 170 floppy disks) depending on whether you have a ZIP 100 MB drive or a ZIP 250 MB drive.

▪ There are two types of ZIP drive: internal ZIP drives and external ZIP drives:

- an internal ZIP drive (a) resides in the main unit, generally under the floppy drive.

- an external ZIP drive (b) is contained in a separate casing that you can connect to your main unit via a parallel port (c) or a USB port (d): thus, you can install a ZIP drive on different computers with a minimum of fuss. The external ZIP drive is supplied with:
  - a cable to connect the drive to your computer (c) or (d),
  - a mains power cable,
  - a ZIP disk,
  - an installation CD-ROM containing an application that allows you to use all the features of the ZIP drive.

*You can use the scanner to enter your photos into your computer in digital format, so that you can send it to your friends, or even modify the image.*

## SCANNERS

- You can use a scanner to copy (scan) a paper document (such as a text or a photo) onto your hard disk, as a digital file. You can then print the image, fax it, send it to your friends by e-mail or even modify it using image-editing software such as Photoshop or PaintShop Pro.

- The scanner is supplied with:
  - a mains power cable (220 VAC),
  - a cable to connect the device to your computer; this can be one of three types: parallel, USB or SCSI (pronounced "scuzzy").
  - an installation CD-ROM containing the scanner driver that allows the operating system to recognise the scanner.
  - image editing software.

Nowadays, some printers also act as scanners. However they accept only one-page documents. On the other hand, you can use a flat-bed scanner to scan from a book.

# Other external devices

As the section above indicates, you can scan your photos into your computer. Alternatively, instead of taking a photo on paper, you can produce your photo directly with a digital camera in the form of a digital file, which you can then transfer onto your hard disk. This type of device is very useful as an independent means of producing your photos.

## DIGITAL CAMERAS

- You can use a digital camera to take photos that you can save on your computer to edit them or simply to print them, to send them to your friends by e-mail or to publish them on your personal web site.

- A digital camera is usually equipped with:

    - a removal storage medium to store your pictures, such as a memory card. Memory cards have capacities ranging from 2 to 64 MB. For example, 8 MB corresponds to 18 photos in SHQ, 36 photos in HQ or 32 photos in standard quality. You can reuse this memory card indefinitely.

    - a drive that you can connect to your computer via the USB connection, to transfer your pictures into your computer.

    - a software application that allows you to view and edit these pictures.

- Digital cameras have similar features to traditional cameras, with:

    - different lenses (36 mm, 140 mm and so forth),

    - exposure control (shutter aperture and speed etc.),

    - flash features (red eye reduction, automatic flash).

 **Most digital cameras provide a small screen for viewing your photo.**

Getting to know the hardware

*Joysticks are an alternative to the keyboard and are generally used to control arcade-type games such as racing circuits or flight simulators.*

## JOYSTICKS

- ▓ The joystick is an input device, as it transmits information to your computer's main unit.

- ▓ Joysticks are essentially used with video games. They replace the use of arrow keys and other keyboard shortcut keys. For example, the joystick provides a firing button, so you do not need to use the space key for this purpose, while another button provides a jump. However, it is not always easy to define these correspondences between the keyboard and the joystick.

- ▓ The joystick is supplied with:

  - a connection to the main unit,
  - a CD-ROM containing the installation software.

 Joysticks reduce keyboard wear and the damage that can occur when players are over-excited!

# 2ⁿᵈ Part

*Now that you know what makes up your computer, you are ready to discover the operating system (Windows XP in this case). This is the working environment in which you will carry out all the tasks on your computer.*

## Discovering the XP environment

# The Windows XP desktop

*Windows is the name of the operating system on your Personal Computer. Your computer could not run without this basic software, as it would not be able to start. PCs (Personal Computers) run the Windows system, while Macintosh computers run a different operating system.*

*Windows XP is a multi-user system. This means that you can create several user accounts on it. In this way, several users can work on the same computer and each user can customise his/her workspace, without affecting the workspaces of the other users. Each user has an individual **My Documents** folder in which to the documents that he/she creates. The user can decide to allow, or not allow other users to access this folder.*

## STARTING WINDOWS XP

▨ When you start your computer, by default, the users of your computer appear in the Windows XP Welcome screen.

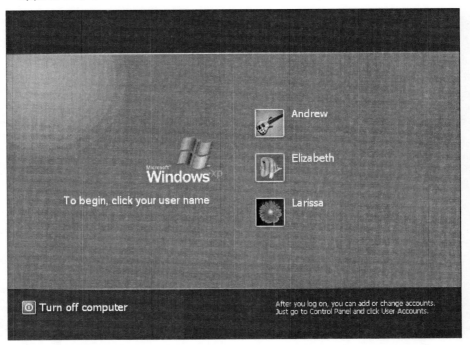

In the above example, three users have been created.

If you are the only user of the computer (if you have just bought your computer or if you have not yet created other user profiles, for example) then this screen will not appear: Windows XP will open your working session automatically and you will go straight into the Windows desktop. In this case, you can skip the rest of this section and go straight on to the next section, **Discovering the XP desktop**.

If several users have been created and you do not see the Windows XP Welcome screen, it means that this screen has been deactivated. In this case, to log on to the computer, you must enter your user name, and any password you may have, in the **Log On to Windows** dialog box.

▨ Otherwise, to log on, click your user name on the Welcome screen, as it prompts you to, then enter any password you may have. If you have forgotten your password, click the ![] button to view any text you entered as a hint when you defined your password: this text should help you to remember your password.

*When you enter your password, it appears as a set of dots.*

▨ When you have finished entering your password, click the ➡ button or press the Enter key to validate it.

**Your workspace or desktop appears on the screen.**

# The Windows XP desktop

*When you have logged on to your computer, the Windows desktop appears on the screen. This desktop provides access to the different items on your computer (it allows you to start Word or Works for example, or to access the files on your hard disk, etc.). The example below shows the desktop by default. However, as you can customize it, your desktop may appear differently.*

## DISCOVERING THE WINDOWS XP DESKTOP

- However, your desktop will always show the following items:
  - the **taskbar** (a) provides a button to access each open application (in the above example, no applications have yet been opened). You can set the taskbar to hide itself when you are not using it or to show the Quick Launch bar, etc.
  - the **start** button (b) provides access to the main Windows menu.
  - the **notification area** (c) displays the system time along with a number of notification icons. For example, it may show an icon to let you know that you have received e-mail.

- the **RecycleBin** (d) is there to receive the files you delete. By default, when you delete a file, the system transfers it to the **RecycleBin**. This approach allows you to retrieve any files you deleted by mistake.

**The desktop may also show other icons (objects) such as shortcuts, which provide quick access to applications or files.**

*You can generally access the different items on your computer in a number of different ways. For example, you may be able to start an application (such as Word or Excel) directly from your desktop, if it shows the corresponding icon. Otherwise, you can always start applications from the start menu.*

## START MENU

▓ To display the Windows XP **start** menu, click the **start** button. Alternatively, you can press the ⊞ key or press ⌈Ctrl⌉⌈Esc⌉ on your keyboard.

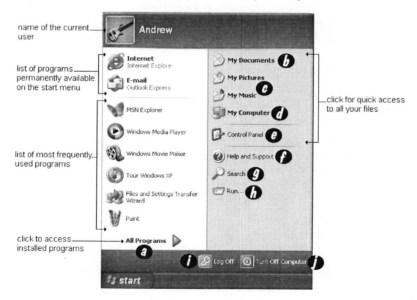

▓ By default, the main Windows XP **start** menu contains the following items:

- The **All Programs** menu (a) lists all the applications installed on the computer.

**Discovering the XP environment**

- The **My Documents** option (b) opens a window of the same name that contains two folders, by default: **My Music** and **My Pictures**. It is recommended that each user of the computer saves his/her documents in his/her **My Documents** folder.
- The **My Music** and **My Pictures** options (c) provide direct access to the corresponding folders.
- The **My Computer** option (d) provides access to all the components of your computer. These components are divided into different categories that depend on how your computer is set up.
- The **Control Panel** option (e) opens a window of the same name that allows you to modify your working environment (by setting up your network connections, managing the user accounts, configuring your devices, adding or removing programs and so forth).
- The **Help and Support** option (f) provides access to the Windows XP **Help and Support Center** application.
- The **Search** option (g) provides access to a number of options that allow you to find files, folders, people (in an address book) and computers on the network. As its name suggests, you can use the **Search the Internet** option in the **Search Companion** bar to carry out a search on the Internet.
- The **Run** option (h) allows you to run a program by specifying the corresponding executable file.
- The **Log Off** option (i) closes the current session and allows another user to log on.
- The **Turn Off Computer** option (j) opens the **Turn off computer** dialog box. This dialog box allows you to turn off your computer, to restart it or to put it into hibernation (Windows XP saves your desktop environment onto your hard disk before turning off your computer, so it can restore your desktop as you left it when you restart your computer).

▨ If you open the **start** menu by mistake, you can close it again by clicking anywhere on the desktop or by pressing Esc.

This chapter does not describe all the menus and options that the **start** menu provides. It concentrates on essential features. Feel free to explore the options and submenus yourself.

*Windows XP opens a session for each user who logs on. When the user logs off, he/she closes his/her session along with all the files and applications opened. It is recommended to close all open sessions before switching the computer off.*

## CLOSING A WINDOWS XP SESSION (LOGGING OFF)

▓ Click the **start** button followed by the **Log Off**  button.

▓ In the **Log Off Windows** dialog box that appears, click the **Log Off** button.

*If you leave a file open without saving modifications you have made to it, this type of message appears.*

▓ If you see this type of message and you want to save your changes, click the **Yes** button. Otherwise, click the **No** button.

Windows saves your settings then displays the Welcome screen (or the **Log On to Windows** dialog box) to allow you to log on again. ENI Publishing provides a more advanced book in the Way In collection called Windows XP - Home Edition that describes how to create a new user account.

 If several people are logged on to your computer, they must all log off before you switch off the computer.

*To switch on your computer, you need only press its **Power** button. On the other hand, if you want to switch off your computer, you must first close any applications that are currently running.*

## SWITCHING OFF YOUR COMPUTER

▓ Close all current sessions (cf. Closing a Windows XP session (logging off)).

▓ Click the **Start** button followed by the **Turn Off Computer** button.

The **Turn off computer** dialog box appears.

The **Cancel** button of this dialog box cancels this action.

The **Restart** button (⁂) shuts down Windows and re-opens it immediately
afterwards, while the **Hibernate** button (⏻) shuts down Windows after saving your
desktop environment onto your hard disk (for example, it saves to your hard disk, the
layout of the windows on the screen and the state of any open applications so that it
can open them in the same state the next time you restart your computer).

▩ Click the **Turn Off** button (⏼) to close Windows so that you can switch off
your computer.

▩ According to the type of computer, your computer will switch itself off
automatically or Windows will advise you that it is safe to switch off your
computer. In the latter case, press the **Power** button on the main unit of
your computer (you may need to keep this button pressed in for several
seconds before the computer switches off).

If any other users are still logged on when you attempt to shut down Windows, this message will appear:

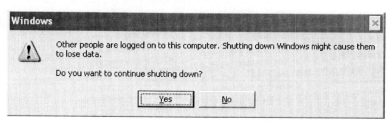

If you click **Yes**, you might lose data; if you click **No**, you will cancel your action.

# Basic operations

*Once you have started your computer, you will not be content just to sit and admire your desktop! To start using your computer and set up your documents, you must open an application (or program). For example, if you want to write a letter, you may want to use a word processor such as Word, or if you want to make calculations, you may want to use a spreadsheet application such as Excel. To access an application you must be able to see it on the screen: you can then "start" or "run" the application.*

## STARTING AN APPLICATION FROM THE START MENU

- Click the **start** button to open the main menu of Windows XP.
- If necessary, point to the **All Programs** option.
- If necessary, move the mouse pointer, to open the appropriate menu or submenu.
- Click the name of the application you want to run.

  **The application window opens and the application's button appears on the taskbar:**

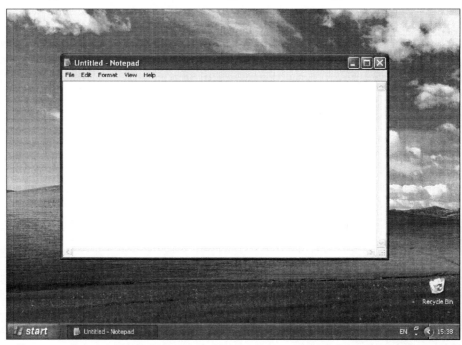

*For example, to start the **Notepad** application, click the **start** button, point to the **All Programs** option then to the **Accessories** menu and click the **Notepad** option.*

The **Notepad** application is installed automatically when you install Windows: it allows you to write text with very simple formatting. If there is a **Notepad** icon on your desktop, you can also double click this icon to start the application (for this reason these icons are called shortcuts).

Programs that you have used recently may appear directly in the **start** menu. To run one of these programs, just open the **start** menu and click the name of the application.

*Every application appears in its own window. The window is the basic element of the Windows system (hence its name). All windows have a number of common items, with which you must be familiar.*

## GENERAL WINDOW ITEMS

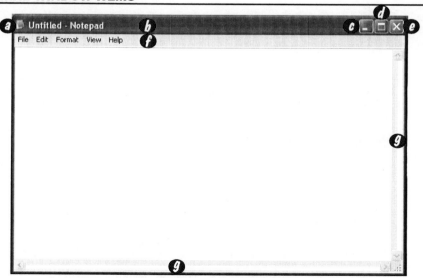

*The scroll bars (g) appear greyed-out because the window is empty.*

Discovering the XP environment

* Every window has the following items:
  - **Control** menu (a): open this menu to manage the window (by moving it or changing its size). In practice, this menu is hardly ever used, as you can carry out the actions it offers in more direct ways.
  - **Title bar** (b): displays the name of the active document (in the above example, this "title" is **Untitled**, as this new document has not yet been saved to disk), followed by the name of the application (Notepad in this example).
  - **Minimize** (c) and **Maximize** (d) buttons: collapse the window into its scroll bar button and enlarge the window to the full screen size, respectively.
  - **Close** button (e): closes the window and the application.
  - **Menu bar** (f): contains the different menus of the application; these menus are closed in this example.
  - **Scroll bars** and **scroll cursors** (g): allow you to scroll through the contents of the window (the **scroll cursors** or **scroll boxes** do not appear in this example because the window is empty).

**When you open a document, such as a letter you have already prepared, it appears in a document window within the application window.**

*When you start a program, the application window may fill the screen (in this case it is said to be in "full-screen" mode). When an application window does not fill the screen, you can see the desktop in the background. If a window is in your way, you can resize it to make it smaller or move it to a more convenient position.*

## MOVING AND RESIZING A WINDOW

* To move a window, point to its title bar (b) then hold down the mouse button, drag to the required position and release the mouse button.
* To minimize the window (into its taskbar button) leaving the application active, click the ▢ button (c).

Here, the **Notepad** application window has been minimized.

* To restore one of your active windows, click its button on the taskbar.

▨ To enlarge the window so that it fills the screen, click the **Maximize** button (▨) on the window's title bar.

**The window now covers the whole screen: only the taskbar remains visible (and you can hide this if you wish). The ▨ button is replaced by the Restore Down button (▨).**

▨ To restore the window to its previous size, click the ▨ button.

▨ To change the height or width of a window that is not in full-screen mode, point to one of the edges of the window: to change the height <u>and</u> the width of the window, point to one of the corners of the window.

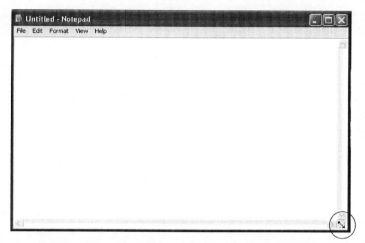

*The mouse pointer appears as a double-headed arrow.*

Hold down the mouse button and drag the mouse to resize the window as required, then release the mouse button.

# Basic operations

*As you can run several applications at once, you can have several open windows that overlap each other. From time to time, you may need to "tidy your desktop".*

## MANAGING SEVERAL WINDOWS

▓ When several windows overlap, you can recognise the active window by the colour of its title bar. By default, the title bar of the active window is blue (while the title bars of inactive windows are light blue) and the taskbar button of the active application appears pressed-in.

*For example, after you have started **Notepad**, run the **Calculator** application by clicking the **start** button, pointing to the **All Programs** option then to the **Accessories** menu and clicking **Calculator**.*

▓ To access a window and activate the corresponding application, click in the window if it is visible, or click its button on the taskbar, or hold down the ⬚Alt key and press the ⬚ key once or more until you select the icon corresponding to the window concerned.

**The active window appears in the foreground.**

Discovering the XP environment

▓ To modify the window layout, right-click an empty space on the taskbar to view the menu that is associated with it:

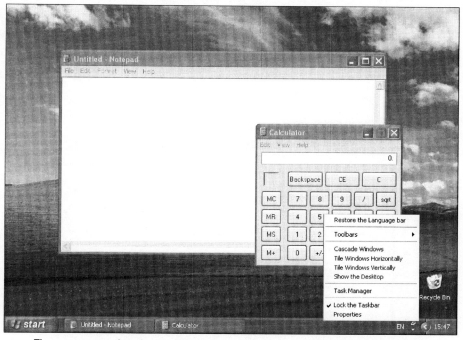

*The menu associated with the taskbar is called the taskbar's shortcut menu.*

▓ Choose one of the following options:

**Cascade Windows**      to arrange the windows so that they overlap each other.

**Tile Windows Horizontally**      to arrange the windows so that they appear one underneath the other.

**Tile Windows Vertically**      to arrange the windows so that they appear side by side.

▓ To minimize all the windows into their taskbar buttons, right-click an empty space on the taskbar and click the **Show the Desktop** option.

▓ To restore all the windows you minimized when you chose the **Show the Desktop** option, display the taskbar shortcut menu and click the **Show Open Windows** option.

This action will restore your previous window layout.

# Basic operations

*You have started your application and perhaps maximized the application window to have as much space as possible: you are now ready to start working. According to the application you are using, you may start entering text or making calculations or doing a drawing. Whatever the application you are using, sooner or later you will need to use the menus that appear under the window's title bar. When you start the application, these menus are closed. To use one of these menus, you must start by opening it.*

## MANAGING AN APPLICATION'S MENUS AND OPTIONS

▥ To open a menu, click its name on the menu bar.

**The menu's options appear:**

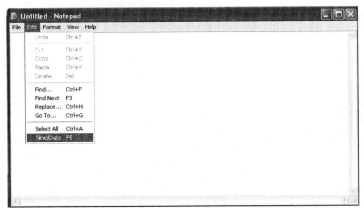

*For example, to open Notepad's **Edit** menu, click **Edit**.*

**You cannot use the greyed-out options, as they are unavailable at the present time.**

**An ellipsis (...) to the right of an option indicates that you will see a dialog box when you choose the option.**

▥ To open an adjacent menu, point to its name.

▥ To activate a menu option, slide the mouse up or down (without clicking) until you are pointing to the option, then click.

▥ To close a menu without activating one of its options, click elsewhere in the window.

■ To access the menu bar from the keyboard, press the `Alt` key or the `F10` key.

**This action selects the first menu on the menu bar, without opening it. One letter in each menu name appears underlined.**

■ To select an adjacent menu, press the `→` key or the `←` key. To open a menu that you have selected, press the `Enter` key or the `↓` key.

■ To open a menu directly, hold down the `Alt` key and press the underlined (mnemonic) letter for the menu concerned.

**For example, in Notepad, the `Alt` E key combination opens the Edit menu.**

■ To activate a menu option, use the `→`, `←`, `↑` and/or `↓` keys to select the option then press the `Enter` key. Alternatively you can simply press the underlined letter for the option concerned (after having opened the menu concerned using one of the techniques described above).

**For example, in Notepad, use the `Alt` E key combination to open the Edit menu then press D to activate the Time/Date option.**

Here are a few commonly-used terms and expressions: a **menu** is made up of **options**. To **run** (or **use**) **a command** means to open the appropriate menu and activate the option concerned: for example, to run the **File - Page Setup** command means to open the **File** menu and click the **Page Setup** option.

The shortcut key (key combination) shown to the right of some menu options allows you to run the option concerned without opening the menu. For example, in **Notepad**, the `F5` function key inserts the time and date into your document without you having to open the **Edit** menu and click the **Time/Date** option.

# Basic operations

With some menu options a small new window may appear on your screen. With these menu options, an ellipsis (...) appears to the right of the option name indicating that the application needs further information before it can complete the action you require. For example, with the **File - Page Setup** command, you must indicate the paper format and orientation in which you want to print. These small windows are called dialog boxes. When a dialog box opens you must close it before you can return to your document and continue working on it.

## FILLING IN DIALOG BOXES

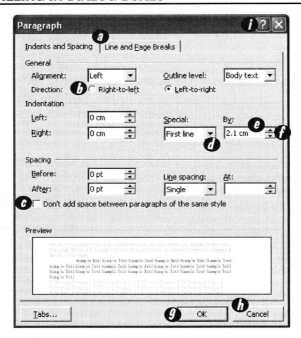

This dialog box was chosen as an example because it offers more features than that which appears when you run the **File - Page Setup** command in the **Notepad** application.

※ A dialog box can contain the following items:

- Tabs (a): provide access to the different pages in the dialog box.
- Option buttons (b): allow you to choose between different exclusive options; a black dot indicates the active option. Only one option can be active at the same time in the same group (such as the **Direction** group in the example).
- Check boxes (c): a tick in the check box indicates that the option is active; to activate or deactivate the option, click the check box.

- List boxes (d): allow you to choose from a list (the example shows a drop-down list box). Click the ▼ button to open the list box and choose a list item; click this button again to close the list box. An ordinary list box sometimes provides a scroll bar and arrows that you can use to scroll through the list contents (as in a window).

- Text boxes (e): allow you to enter information; if the text box accepts numbers it may contain increment buttons (f) that you can click to increase or decrease the displayed value.

- **OK** button (g): closes the dialog box, keeping any changes you have made to the different options.

- **Cancel** button (h): closes the dialog box, cancelling any changes you have made to the different options (clicking this button has the same effect as clicking the ☒ button).

- **Apply** button: sometimes appears in dialog boxes; it allows you to view the effects of your changes without closing the dialog box.

- ？ button: allows you to view specific help information on the different items in the dialog box (see below).

▦ If your mouse breaks down, you can change the options in a dialog box using the keyboard. To access the different options you can use the ⇆ and Shift ⇆ keys; alternatively you can hold down the Alt key and press the letter that appears underlined for the option concerned.

▦ To move between the different options in a group or in a list, use the →, ←, ↑ and/or ↓ keys.
To activate or deactivate a check box, press the space bar.

*When you start an application, it appears in its own window. The easiest way to close an application is to close its window.*

## LEAVING AN APPLICATION (CLOSING A WINDOW)

▦ To close an application, click the ☒ button in the top right-hand corner of the application window or press the Alt F4 keys. Alternatively you can run the **File - Exit** command.

If the application window is minimized (if it appears only as a button on the taskbar) right-click its taskbar button and click the **Close** option.

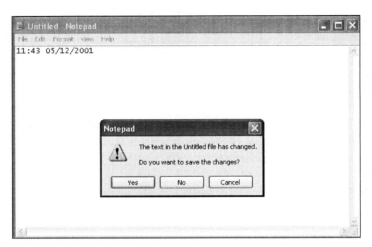

*If you try to close an application without saving all the changes you have made to your document, Windows asks you if you want to save your changes before closing the window.*

Click **Yes** to save your document, click **No** to close the application without saving your changes or click **Cancel** to cancel your action (in this case your document will stay open).

The next chapter explains how to save your documents.

 In general, documents open in document windows (within the application window). To close a document window, click the ☒ button in the top right-hand corner of the document window or press `Ctrl` `F4` (and not `Alt` `F4`) or run the **File - Close** command (and not the **File - Exit** command).

Discovering the XP environment

*Good knowledge of Windows is essential but you also need to work in different applications for different tasks, such as a spreadsheet, a word processor and so on. Here you will learn the basic functions of the Word word processing application and the spreadsheet included in the Works software suite.*

# 3rd Part

# Getting to know Word and Works

# Word: a word processor

*Word is a word processor. A word processor is an application that you can use to create, edit and print letters, reports and so forth. As the previous part described, you must first start (or run) an application before you can use it.*

## STARTING MICROSOFT WORD

▧ Click the **start** button on the taskbar at the bottom of the screen then point the mouse to the **All Programs** option.

**The contents of the All Programs menu appear on the screen.**

▧ Click the **Microsoft Word** option.

**A introductory screen appears presenting the name of the application then the workscreen appears.**

 As with all applications, Word's features develop with each successive version: this chapter describes Word 2002 (the latest version that was available at the time of going to press). If you have an earlier version of Word (Word 2000 or Word 97) your screens will be slightly different from those presented here, but the basic operations that this chapter describes will generally be the same.

 If there is a **Microsoft Word** shortcut icon on your desktop, you can also double-click this icon to start the application.

Getting to know Word and Works

The Word application appears in a window with whose layout you should already be familiar. However, this chapter will describe this window again to help you to get to know it better: remember that all applications use the same basic window layout.

## GETTING STARTED WITH THE WORKSCREEN

The Word workscreen contains various items:

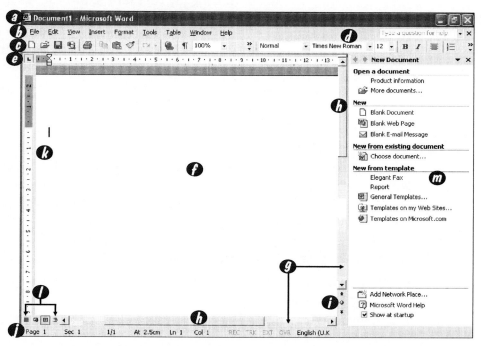

**The title bar and its icons (a)**: on the left is Word's **Control** menu icon (🔲) followed by the name of the active document (here, **Document1** as it is a new document), followed by the name of the application (**Microsoft Word**). On the right, the **Minimize** button (🔲) reduces the window to its minimum size, into the taskbar, without closing the application; the **Restore Down** button 🔲 reduces the window so that it does not necessarily occupy the whole screen. When you click the Restore Down button the **Maximize** button 🔲 appears in its place; this button restores the window to full screen mode. Finally the **Close** button 🔲 closes either the application or just the current document.

# Word: a word processor

**The menu bar (b)** contains the names of the various menus in the Word application and the **Ask a Question** box. You can type a question or a keyword in this box to see the corresponding help topics. The document's **Close** button (⊠) is to the right of this box.

**The Standard (c) and Formatting (d) toolbars** share the same line. You can use these toolbars to run quickly and easily some general Word commands, such as saving a document to disk. If these toolbars do not appear on your screen, you can activate the **Standard** and **Formatting** options in the **View - Toolbars** menu.

**The ruler (e)** lets you change the presentation of your text quickly. Show the ruler using **View - Ruler**.

**The work area (f)** is the space in which you enter and format your text.

**The scroll bars and cursors (g)/(h)**: the cursors in the scroll bars indicate the position of the insertion point in the document and allow you to view text that is longer or wider than the screen.

**The Select Browse Object button (i)** allows you to move around the document according to the items it contains. You can move, for example, from field to field or from end note to end note.

**The status bar (j)** contains information about the Word environment or the selected command.

**The selection bar (k)** is a column that runs down the left of the document.

**The View buttons (l)** show the current document view and allow you to switch to a different view (Normal, Web Layout, Print Layout or Outline).

**The task pane (m)** contains options for carrying out different tasks such as creating a new document, finding text, inserting clipart or creating a mail merge. By default, the **New Document** pane is open when you start Word. You can display the task pane using **View - Task Pane**.

*It is time to start your first text: this is called "entering" your text. Be careful: a word processor does not work in quite the same way as a typewriter! Although entering text may be fairly simple, you must still follow certain rules.*

## ENTERING TEXT

- To enter text in a document, click where you want to start.

- Type in your text. Word takes care of the line breaks: when the insertion point reaches the end of the line Word brings it back to the beginning of the next line automatically.

- To enter text in capitals, press the `Caps Lock` key to set the **Caps Lock** then enter your text as you would normally. To cancel the **Caps Lock**, either press the `Caps Lock` key again or press the `Shift` key, then carry on entering your text.

- To enter a single capital letter, at the beginning of a sentence for example, hold down the `Shift` key while you enter the letter concerned.

- To enter numerical values using the number pad, check that the **Num Lock** indicator is lit (if it is not lit, press the `Num Lock` key) then enter the numbers.

- When you enter the first characters of today's date, a day of the week, a month or certain set expressions that Word recognises, Word displays a ScreenTip showing the full expression (this is Word's autocomplete feature): either press the `Enter` key to accept Word's suggestion or just carry on typing.

- To start a new paragraph, press the `Enter` key.

  The insertion point goes to the beginning of the next line. Your new paragraph will be aligned in the same way as the previous one.

- To leave space between two paragraphs, press the `Enter` key once or more.

  Each time you press the `Enter` key, you create a new empty paragraph.

- Enter the text of your new paragraph.

- Carry on in this way until you have entered all your paragraphs of text.

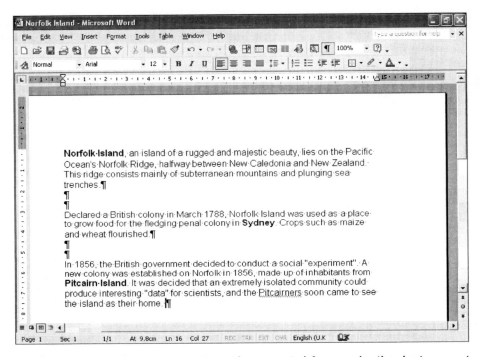

This text is made up of three paragraphs separated from each other by two empty paragraphs. This screen shows the end of paragraph symbol ¶ that marks each place you press the Enter key. The empty spaces at the top, on the left and on the right of the text are the margins that Word will apply when you print the document.

You can format your text either while you are entering it or after you have entered it. For example, you could change the alignment of a paragraph before you enter the text it must contain.

If Word underlines any of the words in your text in red, examine them carefully: they may contain spelling mistakes.

*The great advantage of a word processor over a typewriter is that with a word processor you can change any text you have entered, at any time. For example, if you forget a word in a sentence, there is no cause for alarm! You need only add the missing word in the appropriate place, provided that Insert mode is active!*

## USING INSERT/OVERTYPE MODE

When **Insert** mode is active, Word inserts any characters you enter between the existing characters. When you are in **Overtype** mode, new characters replace (or overtype) the existing ones.

▨ Before you enter the word you want to insert, check that the **OVR** indicator on the status bar appears in grey. If it appears in black, double-click this **OVR** indicator or press the ⌨Ins key.

▨ Enter the word(s) you want to insert.

▨ To deactivate insert mode and activate overwrite mode press the ⌨Ins key or double-click the **OVR** indicator again.

   **The letters OVR on the status bar change from grey to black. They indicate that you are now in overtype mode: the characters you enter replace existing characters.**

▨ To return to insert mode press the ⌨Ins key or double-click the **OVR** indicator again.

*To shift to the right the next word you want to enter, resist the temptation of adding a number of spaces. If you subsequently change part of your document before this point, your text may no longer be correctly aligned. It is much better to insert a tab.*

## INSERTING A TAB

▨ Enter any text that must appear at the beginning of the line.

▨ To go to the next tab stop press the ⌨ key.

   **The insertion point moves to the right.**

▨ To return to the previous tab stop, delete the preceding tab character by pressing the ⌨ key.

# Word: a word processor

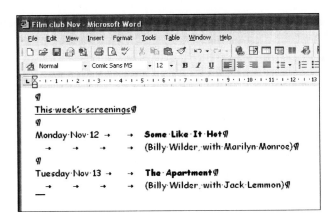

*This example shows two tabs before the name of each film. This technique ensures that the name and the information below it will be perfectly aligned (this would not be the case had spaces been used instead).*

By default, Word sets tab stops every 1.27 cm (or 1/2 inch). They are visible under the ruler as little grey vertical lines. When you show the nonprinting characters, Word represents the tab with the → symbol.

*As indicated above, the main advantage of the word processor is that you can use it to change text without crossing things out. For this, you need to know how to delete text.*

## DELETING TEXT

▨ Click to place the insertion point where you want to delete the text or select the text you want to delete (see "Moving the insertion point" and "Selecting text").

▨ To delete the character immediately before the insertion point, press the ⬅ key.

▨ To delete the character immediately after the insertion point, press the Del key.

▨ To delete a selected piece of text, press the Del key.

▨ To split a paragraph in two, place the insertion point just before what must become the first character of the new paragraph and press the Enter key.

▨ To merge two adjacent paragraphs, place the insertion point at the end of the first paragraph then press the Del key so as to delete the end of paragraph mark that separates the two paragraphs.

*As your text grows, you will need to move around in it, to edit it. For this purpose, you can use the navigation keys or the slide bars on the sides of the Word window.*

## MOVING THE INSERTION POINT

**The insertion point is represented as a flashing vertical line. It marks your position in the document.**

Use the following keys to move the insertion point around:

| | |
|---|---|
| Next/previous character | → / ← |
| Beginning of the next/previous word | Ctrl → / Ctrl ← |
| End/beginning of the line | End / Home |
| Beginning of the next/previous paragraph | Ctrl ↓ / Ctrl ↑ |
| Bottom/top of the window | Ctrl Alt PgDn / Ctrl Alt PgUp |
| Next/previous window | PgDn / PgUp |
| Beginning/end of the document | Ctrl Home / Ctrl End |

Use the scroll bars to reach the text which interests you:

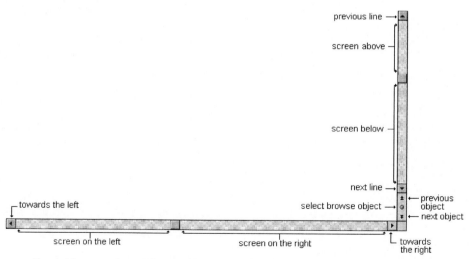

*If your document contains several pages, when you drag the scroll cursor Word displays the number of the current page in a ScreenTip.*

# Word: a word processor

- To go straight to a specific point in the document, drag the scroll cursor along the scroll bar to that point's approximate position.
- Now click in the text to place the insertion point.

 **You cannot go beyond the last characters entered at the end of the file.**

*To apply the same operation to several words, lines or paragraphs, you do not need to work on to each item separately. For example, if you want to move 10 paragraphs you do not need to move the paragraphs one at a time. It is quicker to select the 10 paragraphs concerned then move them all at once.*

## SELECTING TEXT

- To select:

| | |
|---|---|
| a word | double-click the word. |
| a line | point at the left end of the line (the mouse pointer takes the form of an arrow pointing top right) and click once. |
| a paragraph | point at the left of the paragraph (the mouse pointer takes the form of an arrow pointing top right) and double-click. |
| a sentence | point at the sentence, hold down the Ctrl button and click once. |
| the whole document | point at the left edge of the text, and triple-click or hold down the Ctrl button and click once. |

- To select a group of characters:

| | |
|---|---|
| drag | click in front of the first character to be selected and, without releasing the mouse button, move over all the characters required. When the selection is correct, release the mouse button. |
| Shift-click | click in front of the first character that you want to select, hold down the Shift key and click after the last character required. |

If you are using Word 2002, you can select several distinct groups of text, by selecting the first piece of text, holding down Ctrl and selecting the other pieces of text (see example below).

---

**Meals**

**Breakfast** has acquired a certain importance across the Atlantic. If you want to start your day like the locals, which may mean a change from your usual routine, help yourself to fruit juice, crunchy cereal, boiled or fried eggs, served with bacon, or pancakes and sausages, even fresh fruit and cheese. Wash it all down with as much American coffee (weaker than its many European cousins) as you want.

**Lunch** is a much lighter affair, and is generally eaten much faster than breakfast. Choose from innumerable salads, or crudities mixed with cheese and tasty and inventive dressings. You can create your own salad, and eat as much as you like, at the *salad bar*. American beef is generally of good quality. Whether you choose a T-bone steak or a simple hamburger, you will find the meat tasty and well prepared. Be careful, though, as the portions are always very generous. Most meat dishes are served with at least two vegetables. If you like your meat bloody remember to ask for *rare*, or even *extra rare*. You may find that *well done* is a little overdone for your tastes, but asking for *medium* is generally a safe choice. You will find that the choice of meat is much the same as that in the UK.

**Dinner** is a more elaborate meal. If you choose to eat out, and avoid the luncheons, drugstores and fast-food establishments, the service is much more sophisticated, and, of course, the price increases. Restaurants will start to serve dinner from 5 p.m onwards.

The quality of food served in the US, whether it is in a "fast food" establishment or

*Word highlights selected sections. When you make a fresh selection, Word cancels the previous selection.*

---

■ Place the insertion point before the first character you want to select.
Hold down the Shift key as you use the direction keys to select (you can also press Ctrl Shift → to extend your current selection to include the next word).

■ When you are happy with the selection, release the Shift key.

■ To select the whole document, use Ctrl **A** or the **Edit - Select All** command.

*Moving or copying any selection of text is a very useful feature of Word.*

## MOVING/COPYING TEXT

■ Select the block of text you want to move or copy.

■ To move the text, press F2; to copy the text, press Shift F2.
**On the status bar, Word asks "Move to where" for a move or "Copy to where" for a copy.**

■ Place the insertion point where you want to move or copy.

■ Press the Enter key.

- ▓ Select the block of text you want to move or copy.

- ▓ Point to the selected text.

- ▓ If you want to copy the text, hold down the [Ctrl] key and drag so as to position the vertical grey line where you want to copy the text.

- ▓ If you want to move the text, simply drag to the position where you want to move the text.

   **As you move text, a rectangle accompanies the mouse pointer; as you copy text a second rectangle containing a plus sign accompanies the mouse pointer.**

*For the moment, your document is in the computer's central memory and nowhere else (in the RAM, which the first chapter described). If your computer powers down suddenly your document will disappear. To save your document you must save it onto the hard disk of your computer.*

## SAVING A NEW DOCUMENT

- ▓ **File - Save** or 🖫 or [Ctrl] **S**

   The **Save As** dialog box appears. By default, Windows saves documents in the folder called **My Documents**.

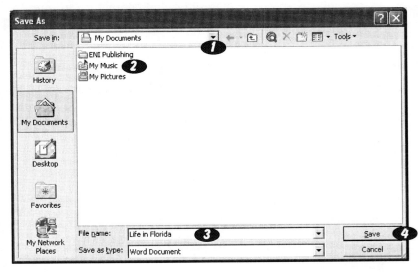

*1.* If you do not want to save your file in the folder that the **Save in** box suggests, click the arrow to open this list then choose the drive you want to use (for example, the C: icon generally represents your hard disk) and/or choose the folder that must accommodate your file (such as **Anne's Documents**, or **Shared Documents**, which all users can access).

*2.* If necessary, double-click the name of the folder in which you want to save your file: the name of this file appears in the **Save in** box.

*3.* In the **File name** box, enter the name you want to give to your document: a document name can be up to 255 characters long and can contain spaces (on the other hand it cannot contain \ / : < > or | characters).

*4.* Click to save your document.

**The name of the document appears in the title bar. The name extension may also appear: a Word document has always a .doc name extension, even if it is not always visible on the screen.**

You can use the **File - Save As** command to save your current document under a different name.

# Word: a word processor

Getting to know Word and Works

*When you want to continue working on a file you started yesterday for example, you must open your file from your hard disk.*

## OPENING A DOCUMENT

▒ **File - Open** or 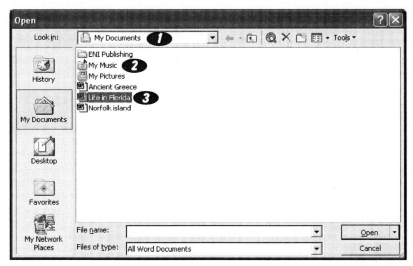 or `Ctrl` **O**

**1.** If the folder that the **Look in** box suggests does not contain the file you want to open, click the arrow to open this list then choose the drive concerned (for example, the **C:** icon generally represents your hard disk) and/or choose the folder that contains your file (such as the folder of another user or **Shared Documents**, which all users can access).

**2.** If necessary, double-click the name of the folder that contains your file.

To access the parent folder, click the ⬆ tool button.

**3.** Double-click the name of the document you want to open or select it then click the **Open** button.

To open one of the last documents you worked on, open the **File** menu and click the document's name at the end of the menu or click the link to the document in the **Open a document** area in the **New Document** task pane.

*As you work on your file, you will change it or add new information to it. You make these changes in the central memory (in the electronic circuits of your computer). You update the computer file on your hard disk each time you save your file. When you open your file, it is always in the state it was in when it was last saved. This means that if a power cut occurs, you will lose any changes you made since you last saved your file.*

## SAVING AN EXISTING DOCUMENT

▨ **File - Save** or ▣ or Ctrl **S**

Windows does not display the **Save As** dialog box as your file already has a name and a storage location. Windows saves only the changes you have made.

*When you have finished working on a file, you can close it so as not to clutter up your computer's memory.*

## CLOSING A DOCUMENT

▨ Activate the document you want to close.

▨ **File - Close** or ✕ or Ctrl **W** or Alt F4

If you try to close a document that you have not yet saved or that you have changed since you last saved it, the following message appears:

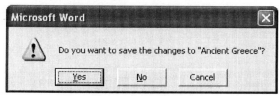

▨ Click the **Yes** button to save your file before you close it or click **No** to close your file without saving it or click **Cancel** not to close your document.

# Word: a word processor

*When you have finished structuring your text, you may want to change its look to make it more pleasant to read or to highlight important words or phrases.*

## FORMATTING CHARACTERS

▨ If you have already entered the characters concerned, select them.

▨ Click one or more of the buttons on the **Formatting** bar to apply the attribute you require: **B** **Bold** type, *I* *Italics*, <u>U</u> <u>Underlined.</u>

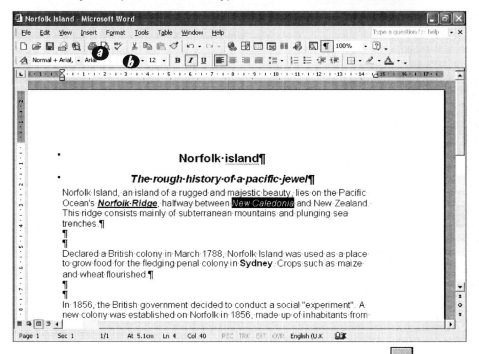

*In this example, italic style has been applied to "New Caledonia". The* ***I*** *button shows a blue border. You can apply several different formatting styles to the same text.*

▨ To deactivate a formatting style, click the corresponding tool button again.

▨ To change the font or the font style, open the corresponding list on the **Formatting** toolbar (a or b) then click the font or the font size you need.

You can format your characters while you type: activate the formatting style you require, enter your text you require in this format then deactivate the formatting style and continue entering your text.

▓ If you have already entered the characters concerned, select them.

▓ Use the following key combinations to apply the attributes you require:

| | |
|---|---|
| `Ctrl` **B** | **Bold** |
| `Ctrl` **I** | *Italic* |
| `Ctrl` **U** | Underlined |
| `Ctrl` `Shift` **D** | Double Underlined |
| `Ctrl` `Shift` **W** | Words only Underlined |
| `Ctrl` `Shift` **K** | SMALL CAPITALS |
| `Ctrl` `Shift` **A** | CAPITALS |
| `Ctrl` `Shift` **+** | in $^{Superscript}$ (use the key on the alphanumerical keyboard) |
| `Ctrl` **=** | in $_{Subscript}$ |
| `Ctrl` `Shift` **H** | Hidden text |

▓ If the characters have already been entered, select them.

▓ **Format - Font** or `Ctrl` **D**

The **Font** dialog box provides the full set of character formatting features.

▓ If necessary, activate the **Font** tab.

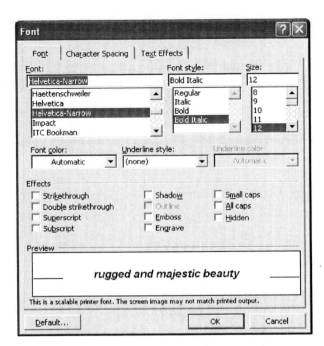

*In the **Preview** box, Word shows the text selected in the format chosen.*

▒ Choose the formatting styles you require from the **Font**, **Font style**, **Size** and **Underline style** lists and from the **Effects** frame.

**The illustration below shows the result of each effect:**

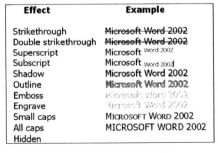

| Effect | Example |
|---|---|
| Strikethrough | Microsoft Word 2002 |
| Double strikethrough | Microsoft Word 2002 |
| Superscript | Microsoft Word 2002 |
| Subscript | Microsoft Word 2002 |
| Shadow | Microsoft Word 2002 |
| Outline | Microsoft Word 2002 |
| Emboss | Microsoft Word 2002 |
| Engrave | Microsoft Word 2002 |
| Small caps | MICROSOFT WORD 2002 |
| All caps | MICROSOFT WORD 2002 |
| Hidden | |

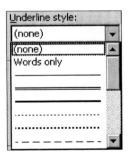

**The Underline Style list offers several possibilities.**

▒ Click **OK** to confirm.

*Now you have formatted your text, you may want to change its presentation by reformatting its paragraphs. This section explains how to align text with the left margin (Word aligns your text in this way by default) with the right margin or between these two margins (this type of alignment is often used for headings). You can even align your text with both of these margins at once (newspapers use this type of alignment and so does this paragraph you are reading).*

## CHANGING TEXT ALIGNMENT IN PARAGRAPHS

▓ Select the paragraphs whose alignment you want to change or if you want to re-align a single paragraph, simply click in it.

▓ According to the alignment you want to apply, click the corresponding button on the **Formatting** toolbar:

 left alignment (by default).

 centre alignment.

 right alignment.

 justified alignment: Word spaces the words out automatically to align the text with the left margin and with the right margin.

▓ Select the paragraphs whose alignment you want to change or if you want to re-align a single paragraph, simply click in it.

▓ **Format - Paragraph**

▓ Open the **Alignment** list then click the option corresponding to the required alignment.

▓ Click the **OK** button.

▓ Select the paragraphs whose alignment you want to change or if you want to re-align a single paragraph, simply click in it.

▓ According to the alignment you want to apply, use one of the following shortcut keys:

⌨ Ctrl **L**    left alignment

⌨ Ctrl **E**    centre alignment

# Word: a word processor

| Ctrl R | right alignment |
| Ctrl J | justified alignment |

 You can also align the text in your paragraphs while you are entering your text. When you finish your current paragraph, press Enter. If the new paragraph requires the same alignment as the previous one, simply keep typing; if you wish to use a different type of alignment, choose the new type then enter the text for that paragraph.

*When you have finished your document, you may want to print it so that you can give it to other people. However, if you preview your whole document before you print it you will get a better result and save ink and paper: the print preview shows your document as Windows will print it.*

## STARTING THE PRINT PREVIEW

▓ **File - Print Preview** or [icon] or Ctrl F2

A reduced image of your document appears, as Word would print it. On the status bar, Word indicates the number of the page it is displaying.

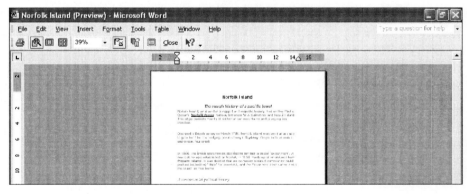

The toolbar shows the current print preview zoom level.

▓ To view other pages of your document, use the vertical scroll bar or move from page to page using the PgUp and PgDn buttons.

▓ To return to the work area, click the **Close** button or press the Esc key.

You can start printing from the preview by clicking the  tool button.

*If you have already checked your document in the print preview or if you have printed your document before, you can start printing without concerning yourself with the page setup or with the print options.*

## PRINTING A DOCUMENT

▓ Click the  tool button.

The printing starts immediately according to the default settings that the **Print** dialog box defines.

*According to the length of your document, you may need several sheets of paper to print it. You can choose to print only that part of the document you have previously selected or only certain pages of your document (for example, suppose that your document will print on 4 pages and that you have just modified only the second page: rather than printing all four pages you can choose to print only the second page).*

## PRINTING PART OF A DOCUMENT

▓ To print a group of paragraphs, select them.

▓ **File - Print** or Ctrl **P**

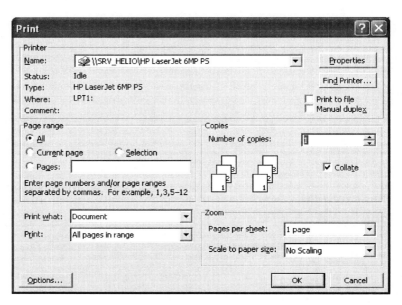

To print the part of your text that you selected previously, click the **Selection** option in the **Page range** frame.

To print only certain pages, access the **Pages** box in the **Page range** frame and enter the number(s) of the page(s) you want to print.

To print a series of consecutive pages, enter the number of the first page then a dash then the number of the last page (for example, to print from page 5 to page 10, enter 5-10).

If the pages you want to print are not consecutive, use commas to separate the page numbers (for example, to print page 5 and page 10, enter 5,10).

To print the page in which the insertion point is currently positioned, activate the **Current page** option.

▓ To print only even or odd pages, select the corresponding option in the **Print** list.

▓ Click **OK** to confirm.

This section covers only Word's basic features. Of course, this highly sophisticated word processor offers many other features (column layouts, tables of contents, indexes, mail merges end so forth). ENI Publishing offers books on Word 2002 in other collections.

# Works: a software suite

*Works often comes with the computer as standard supply. This application groups a word processor (to create and change text documents) a spreadsheet (to create and change tables) and a database management system (to create and use cross-referenced lists for storing data, such as information on catalogue items, for example). Works also includes other tools and applications for managing items such as your address book and your personal accounts. This chapter will describe the working environment that Works offers and the basic features of the spreadsheet application it provides.*

## STARTING MICROSOFT WORKS

You can choose to run one of the applications integrated into Works (such as the spreadsheet, database or word processor), or you can go to a home page, which offers several options (to create a letter or a budget, to open an existing document, etc).

### Starting a Works application

▓ To run one of the Works applications, click the **start** button, choose the **All Programs** option and point to the **Microsoft Works** option that is preceded by the 🔲 symbol.

The contents of the Microsoft Works menu appear on the screen:

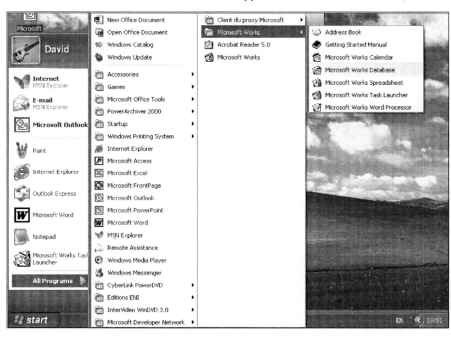

Click the option that corresponds to the program you want to start: the **Address Book**, **Microsoft Works Calendar**, **Microsoft Works Database**, **Microsoft Works Spreadsheet**, **Microsoft Works Word Processor** or **Microsoft Works Task Launcher**.

## Accessing the Task Launcher

Click the **start** button, choose the **All Programs** option and click the other **Microsoft Works** option, the one preceded by the **Task Launcher** icon: 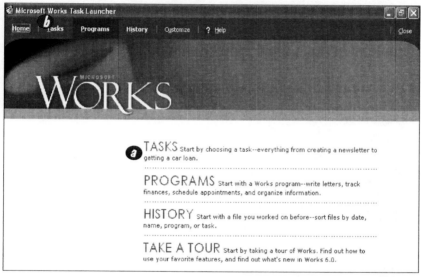.

The Task Launcher **Home** page appears:

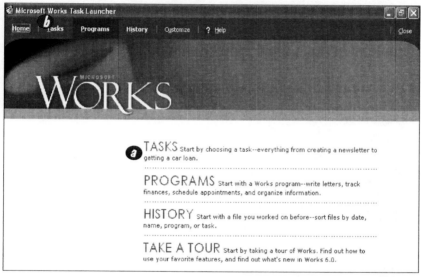

To go to the **Task Launcher**, click the **TASKS** hyperlink that you can see in the centre of the screen (a), or the **Tasks** link on the navigation bar in the top part of the screen (b).

 If you have a shortcut icon on your Windows Desktop, double-click it to start the **Task Launcher**.

# Works: a software suite

*You have started the Task Launcher (see Starting Microsoft Works) and you can now see its interface, which is a bit like a Web page (as you will see in the chapter on the Internet). When you move the mouse around and point to a category, the mouse pointer becomes a hand with a pointing finger. This means that you are pointing at a hyperlink to a task, program or document (hyperlink is also an Internet term). If you click the link, you will open the task, program or document. In fact, the Task Launcher is the general menu for Microsoft Works. Below you can see how to use it.*

## USING THE TASK LAUNCHER

### Launching a task

▒ To start a task, which means create a document using a template with the help of a "wizard":

**1.** Click the **Tasks** link.

**2.** Click the category that best describes the kind of task you want to find.

**3.** Click the task you want to start.

In the right of the window, the **Start this task** option appears.

░ Click **Start this task**.

The wizard window appears. A wizard is a program that guides you through one or more steps to set up the task you have chosen.

░ Click the style of document you want, then click **Next** if the wizard is made up of several steps, or **Finish** if not.

░ If need be, follow the rest of the steps by selecting the options you want, then click **Finish**.

Microsoft Works starts the application that corresponds to the document you are creating.

## Starting an application directly

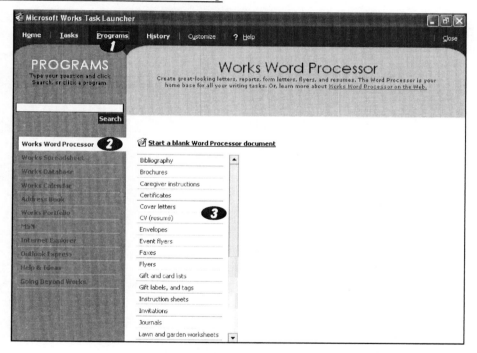

**1.** If necessary, click the **Programs** link in the **Microsoft Works Task Launcher** window.

**2.** Select the program you want. A list of tasks associated with this program appears to the right.

**3.** Click the **Start a blank "document type"** option if you want to open the corresponding application and create an empty document, or choose the task you want to perform, from the task list, and then click the **Start this task** option that appears.

If you use the first technique, a new document opens: if you choose a task, a wizard will help you to create a document using a template.

*If you are working with a document and you want to enter new data, you will have to create a new document.*

## CREATING A DOCUMENT

▨ In any of the Works programs, use **File - New** or press Ctrl **N**.

The **Task Launcher** window appears.

The program name selected in the left part of the screen corresponds to the program you were in when you used **File - New**.

**1.** If necessary, click the name of the program you want.

**2.** Click the **Start a blank "document type"** option.

A new, empty document appears on the screen.

# Getting started with your computer

 Click the tool button if you want to create a new document without returning to the Task Launcher.

To create your first table, you must start the Works Spreadsheet program and open a blank spreadsheet. You can do this via the Windows start menu or with the **Task Launcher**, as described on the previous pages. Like all Windows applications, the spreadsheet appears in a window. All windows have common features, with which you should be familiar.

## DESCRIPTION OF THE SPREADSHEET WINDOW

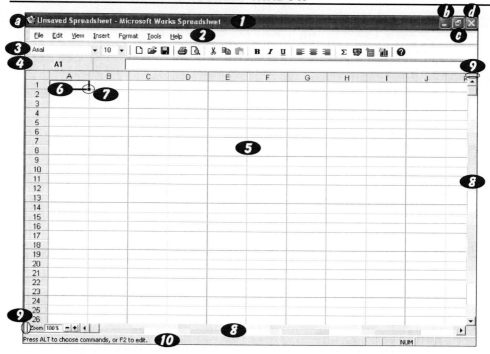

You can see only a small part of the Works spreadsheet, which contains **256 columns** and **16384 rows** (the last cell in the spreadsheet is called cell **IV16384**).

# Works: a software suite

- The **title bar** (1) contains, on the left, the Spreadsheet's control menu icon (a), followed by its name and the name of the active spreadsheet. On the right are the **Minimize** (b), **Maximize** or **Restore** (c) and **Close** (d) buttons.

- The **menu bar** (2) contains all the Spreadsheet application's menus. Each menu provides options that you can use while you are working.

- The **toolbar** (3) supplies tools for carrying out actions or applying formats more rapidly. You can hide or display the toolbar using the **View - Toolbar - Show Toolbar** command.

- The **entry bar** (4) shows the reference of the active cell; this is where you enter and edit data.

- The **work area** (5) is the space in which you work. It is made up of **cells**. The cells are created at the intersection of a column and a row, and their names are made up of the letter of the column and number of the row. When the pointer is in a cell, that cell becomes the **active cell** (6). It is surrounded by a black outline and its reference appears in the left of the entry bar. The black square you can see at the bottom right of the active cell is called the **fill handle** (7).

- The **scroll bars** (8) allow you to scroll the spreadsheet in the window.

- The **split box** (9) is used to split the window.

- The **status bar** (10) contains information about the keyboard or instructions about what you should do.

*So here you are sitting in front of a spreadsheet. Before you can start entering data into the cells, you need to know how to go to the appropriate cell.*

## MOVING AROUND A SPREADSHEET

- Use the scroll bars to display the cell you want to activate then click in it, or use the following keys:

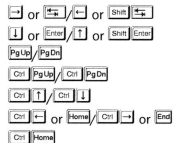

cell to the right/left,

cell below/above,

first/last row on the screen,

screen to the right/left,

first/last row in the active column,

first/last cell in the active row,

Cell A1.

# Getting started with your computer

When you move the mouse pointer around the spreadsheet, the name of the active cell appears at the beginning of the entry bar.

 You can also use **Edit - Go To** or [Ctrl] **G** or [F5], enter the reference of the cell you want, then click **Go to** or press [Enter].

*Now you are ready to create your first table. To create the table's cells, you will have to enter data into the spreadsheet's cells. These data can be of four different kinds: text, numbers, dates (Works knows there is no such date as 32/14/01!), and of course, calculations.*

## ENTERING DATA

▨ Activate the cell that will contain the data.

▨ Type the data. If you make a mistake, undo it by pressing [←].

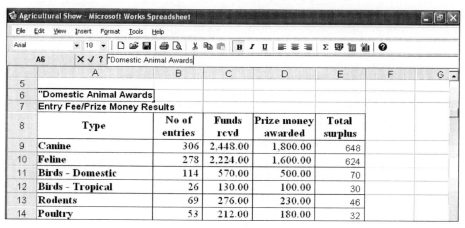

| | A | B | C | D | E | F | G |
|---|---|---|---|---|---|---|---|
| 5 | | | | | | | |
| 6 | "Domestic Animal Awards | | | | | | |
| 7 | Entry Fee/Prize Money Results | | | | | | |
| 8 | Type | No of entries | Funds rcvd | Prize money awarded | Total surplus | | |
| 9 | Canine | 306 | 2,448.00 | 1,800.00 | 648 | | |
| 10 | Feline | 278 | 2,224.00 | 1,600.00 | 624 | | |
| 11 | Birds – Domestic | 114 | 570.00 | 500.00 | 70 | | |
| 12 | Birds – Tropical | 26 | 130.00 | 100.00 | 30 | | |
| 13 | Rodents | 69 | 276.00 | 230.00 | 46 | | |
| 14 | Poultry | 53 | 212.00 | 180.00 | 32 | | |

As soon as you type the first character, three buttons appear on the entry bar:

 (equivalent to [Enter]) confirms the data,

© Editions ENI - All rights reserved

**X** (the same as Esc) cancels the data,

**?** displays the help window.

▦ Confirm the data or activate the next cell.

As soon as they are confirmed, Text data are aligned at the left of the cell and Number and Date data are aligned on the right.

▦ Keep the following points in mind:

- to enter a negative value, precede it with a minus sign (-) or place it between brackets.
- to enter a number as a currency value, type the currency symbol then the number.
- enter a percentage by typing % just after the number.
- to enter decimal values, use the decimal separator specified in your Windows settings (usually the point).
- type times as follows: HH:MM:SS (e.g. 14:30:55).
- for dates, use any of the following formats: 02/02/95, 02/02, 02/95, 2 February 1995, February, 2 February, February 95. For year values entered as two figures, Works interprets them as follows: 00 to 29 correspond to 2000 to 2029, 30 to 99 correspond to 1930 to 1999.

*It is easy to make mistakes as you enter data, so it is a good idea to know how to change a cell's contents.*

## EDITING THE CONTENTS OF A CELL

▦ Activate the cell you want to edit.

The cell contents appear in the entry bar.

▦ Press F2 or double-click in the cell, or click in the entry bar in the appropriate place.

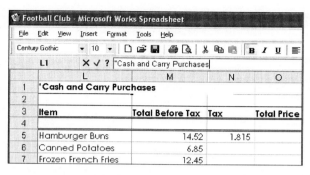

*Text data is preceded by an opening quotation mark (").*

Make the necessary changes (such as adding or deleting characters) then confirm (click ✅ or press ⌜Enter⌟).

*You will often find that you need to change cell contents and sometimes you will want to delete them.*

## DELETING THE CONTENTS OF A CELL

Select the cell(s) concerned and press ⌜Del⌟. If you would rather use the mouse, you can also drag the fill handle over the cells you want to delete.

*The Works Spreadsheet was created to calculate formulas. However, it is not a calculator. If you ask it to calculate (14879/45.5877 + 961413.458/56789.45), you will get an answer, but you would do better to go and find your calculator (or use the Windows **Calculator** application).*

*The formulas that you can enter are based not on the numbers contained in the cells but on the references of the cells themselves. This means that, if you make a change to the cell contents, the result of the formula will be updated automatically, without any intervention on your part.*

## ENTERING A CALCULATION FORMULA

Activate the cell that is to contain the result and type a =.

Move the pointer to the first cell you want to include in the calculation.

Type the mathematical operator to be used:
+ (addition), - (subtraction), * (multiplication), / (division) or ^ (raising to power).

In the same way, activate each cell that is to be included and add the appropriate mathematical operator.

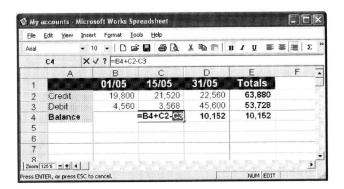

*The calculation formula appears in the entry bar. The selected cell appears with a black background, and the status bar indicates that you are in EDIT mode.*

▦ When you have inserted the last cell, use ☑ or [Enter] to confirm.

The result is visible in the cell, but the true content of the cell is the formula, which you can see in the entry bar when the cell is active. This is why, if you change any of the data in the cells in the formula, the result changes at the same time.

You can also use the keyboard simply to type in the references of the cells that you want to include.

*Works offers an impressive range of formulas, or functions. You can apply these functions to a set of adjoining cells (called a cell range). For example you can calculate the sum of the values they contain, their average or their standard deviation. You can also apply trigonometric functions, to calculate the cosine of an angle, for example.*

### INSERTING A FUNCTION INTO A FORMULA

▦ Activate the cell that is to contain the function.

▦ **Insert - Function**

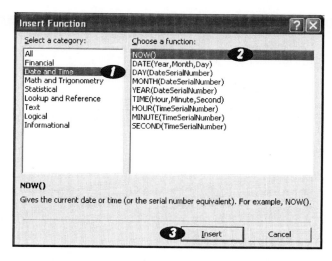

*The NOW() function inserts today's date in the selected cell (this date is then updated automatically).*

***1.*** Under **Select a category**, choose the function you want (choose **All** to see a list of all the functions).

***2.*** Click the name of the function you want to use and a description of the function appears in the bottom of the dialog box.

***3.*** Insert the function into the active cell.

▒ Finish the formula and confirm.

*When you create tables, it is quite common that cells will have the same contents. Rather than taking the time to enter text or formulas over and over again, you can ask Works to reproduce your data in the appropriate cells. This is a technique known as "filling". Whether you are filling 10 or 500 cells, the data appears immediately.*

## COPYING THE CONTENTS OF A CELL TO ADJACENT CELLS

▒ To copy the contents of a cell to the cells below, select the cell whose contents you want to copy and also the destination cells, then use **Edit - Fill Down**.

▒ To copy the contents of a cell to the cells to the right, select the cell in question and also the destination cells and use **Edit - Fill Right**.

▒ If you want to copy a cell's contents to any other cells, activate the cell in question then point to its fill handle so that a cross and the text FILL appear. Now drag the pointer as far as the last destination cell.

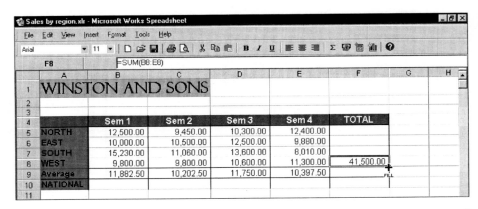

By dragging upwards, you will copy the calculation formula from cell **F8** to the cells above.

*If you have finished your table, but now realise that you have forgotten a row, there is no need to fret. In Works, you can easily insert blank rows and columns between existing ones.*

## INSERTING ROWS/COLUMNS

▒ If you want to insert one row (or column), click in the row (or column) that will come after the new row (or column).

▒ If you want to insert several rows (or columns), select many rows (or columns) as you want to insert.

▒ **Insert - Insert Row** or **Insert Column** or `Ctrl` `Shift` +

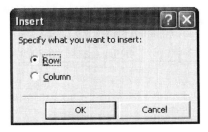

▒ Choose one of these options.

▒ Click the **OK** button.

Works inserts a new row (or column) and moves the selected cells downwards (or to the right).

*Not only can you insert rows and columns, you can also delete any rows or columns that you no longer need.*

## DELETING ROWS/COLUMNS

▨ Select a cell in each row or column you want to delete.

▨ **Insert - Delete Row** or **Delete Column** or `Ctrl` -

Be careful, because Works does not ask for confirmation and immediately deletes the rows or columns and their contents. If you make a mistake, use **Edit - Undo Delete Row** or **Undo Delete Column**.

*If you have typed a long text into a cell, only the first characters will be visible. The rest of the text is not lost however: by increasing the column width, you will be able to see the whole text.*

## CHANGING COLUMN WIDTHS

▨ To increase or decrease the width of a column manually, point to the vertical line you can see to the right of the column letter.

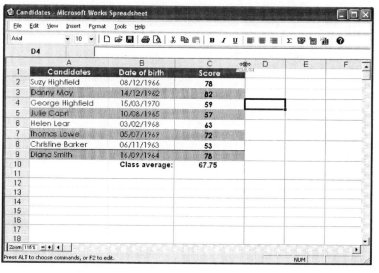

The mouse pointer takes this shape: ADJUST.

▨ Drag to change the column width.

▨ To adjust the column width to fit its contents, double-click the column header.

If you want a set of columns to have the same width, select them and use **Format - Column Width**. In the text box, type the number of characters you want as the column width, then click **OK** to confirm.

When a cell contains numerical data and the column is too narrow to display the entire cell contents, you will see that the numbers are replaced by hash symbols (#). If you increase the column width, the numbers will appear correctly.

*In the same way as you can change the width of columns, you can also change the height of rows.*

## CHANGING ROW HEIGHTS

To change a row's height manually, point to the vertical line under the row's number, so that the mouse pointer takes this shape: then drag.

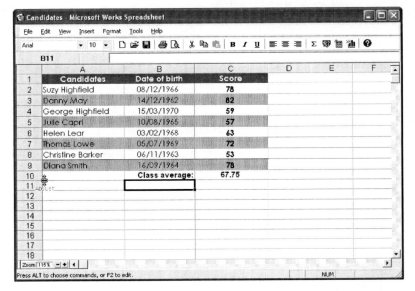

To adjust the row's height to fit its contents, double-click the row number.

If you want several rows to have the same height, select them then use **Format - Row Height**.

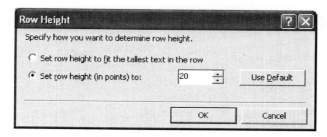

In the text box, enter the number of points you want for the row height.

The **Use Default** button will apply the default height to the selection and the **Set row height to fit the tallest text in the row** option will adjust the selected rows to fit their contents.

▦ Click **OK**.

*After you have entered all the data into your table, you may want to format this data (for example, you may want to use larger characters for your totals).*

## FORMATTING CHARACTERS

▦ Select the cells whose characters you want to format.

▦ To change the font or the font size, click (a) or (b) to open the corresponding list then click the font or the font size you require.

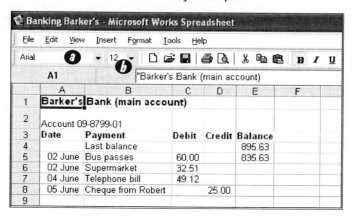

# Works: a software suite

▓ You can choose from the following character styles:

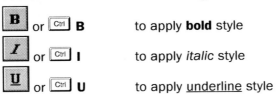

| **B** or Ctrl **B** | to apply **bold** style |
| *I* or Ctrl **I** | to apply *italic* style |
| **U** or Ctrl **U** | to apply underline style |

▓ Repeat the same action on the cell to cancel the style.

▓ Select the cells whose characters you want to format.

▓ **Format - Font**

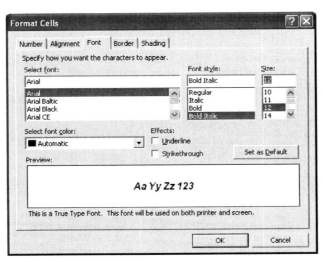

*You need to use this command only to apply **Strikethrough** style and to change the font colour. You can use the **Number** page of this dialog box to format numerical values and the **Border** page to apply a border around selected cells.*

▓ Activate the different formatting options you want to apply to the cells you selected.

▓ Click **OK** to confirm your settings.

*When you start a new document in an application, Windows stores the data you enter in the computer's central memory: if your computer powers down you will lose all this data. So as not to lose this information you must store it on your computer's hard disk. You open, save and close a Works file as you would a Word file. The chapter on Word describes these operations in detail (cf. Saving a new document, Opening a document, Saving an existing document and Closing a document, on pages 68 to 71).*

## SAVING, OPENING AND CLOSING A WORKS DOCUMENT

As with Word, use the following commands for these purposes:

▥ To save the document on which you are working:

**File - Save** or 🖫 or Ctrl **S**

▥ To save the document under a new name:

**File - Save As** or F12

▥ To open a document you saved previously:

**File - Open** or 📂 or Ctrl **O**

▥ To close a document:

**File - Close** or ✕ or Ctrl F4

*You will save paper and ink if you use the print preview, before you print your spreadsheet, this feature will show you a preview of the document exactly as it will print on paper.*

## USING THE PRINT PREVIEW

▥ **File - Print Preview** or 🔍

# Works: a software suite

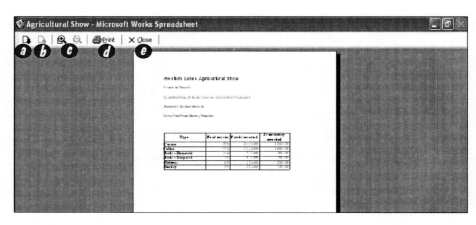

※ Use the following buttons:

    (a)    to see the next page,

    (b)    to see the previous page,

    (c)    to change the zoom,

    (d)    to print the document,

    (e)    to return to the document window.

*If you have already printed your document, or if you have already checked the print preview, you can go ahead and print without worrying about the page layout or the print options.*

## PRINTING A DOCUMENT

※ **File - Print** or `Ctrl` **P**

Getting to know Word and Works

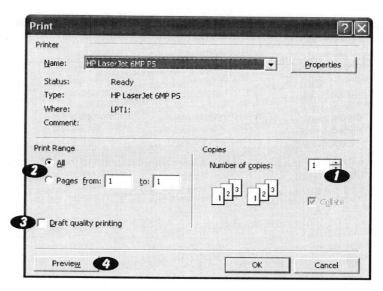

**1.** Indicate how many copies you want.

**2.** In the **Print Range** frame, click **Pages** if you only want to print a selection of pages and, in **from** and **to**, enter the numbers of the first and last pages you want to print.

**3.** In the spreadsheet and the database, you can activate the **Draft quality printing** to speed up the printing (charts, database forms, drawings and so forth will not be printed).

**4.** Click **OK** to start printing, or choose **Preview** if you want to check the print preview.

 Use the ⎙ tool button to print without passing by the **Print** dialog box.

# Works: a software suite

*When you have finished using a Works application, you will want to close it. The way to do this is to close the application window.*

## CLOSING WORKS APPLICATIONS

▓ **File - Exit** or click the ☒ button on the application window, or press ⌨Alt⌨F4.

If you try to leave an application before you save changes you have made to the open document, a message appears to remind you of this situation.

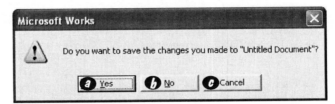

(a)   Saves the document.

(b)   Closes the application without saving the document.

(c)   Keeps the application open.

▓ If your document has never been saved, Works will suggest you save the document and give it a name.

When you work with your word processor or spreadsheet, you save your work as documents, or files. But how do you find your way around the files stored on the computer? How do you delete a file or copy it onto a disk? To carry out this type of task, you can use the Windows Explorer, which you access with the My Documents window.

# 4th
# Part

## Windows Explorer

# My Documents window

For each user of your computer, Windows XP creates an individual folder called **My Documents**, in which the user can store all his/her files (letters, workbooks, pictures and so forth). By default, the **My Documents** folder contains two subfolders: **My Pictures** and **My Music**. These subfolders contain sample pictures and music. Naturally, each user can create other subfolders in his/her **My Documents** folder (cf. Managing folders and files - Creating a folder).

If you wish, you can allow other computer users to access your personal (**My Documents**) folder and its subfolders or you can make these folders private by forbidding all other users from accessing your personal data. If several users can access your computer, Windows XP identifies the different personal folders according to the name of the user concerned. For example, suppose a computer has two users, Beatrice and Benedick: when Beatrice is logged on to the computer, her personal folder is called **My Documents**, while Benedick's personal folder appears under the name of **Benedick's Documents** (Beatrice can view Benedick's personal folder in the **My Computer** window by choosing **start - My Computer**). Windows identifies the **My Pictures** and **My Music** folders in the same way: when Beatrice is logged on to the computer, Benedick's **My Pictures** and **My Music** folders appear under the names of **Benedick's Pictures** and **Benedick's Music**, respectively.

## DISCOVERING THE MY DOCUMENTS WINDOW

▓ To open the **My Documents** window, click the **start** button on the taskbar then click the **My Documents** option.

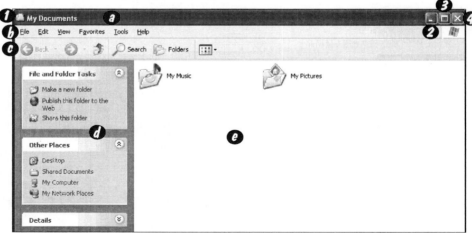

By default, the **My Documents** window contains only the **My Pictures** and **My Music** subfolders. You can create other folders in the **My Documents** folder and thereby add them to this list of existing subfolders.

Windows Explorer

- The **My Documents** window contains the following items:
  - the **title bar** (a): contains the **Control** menu (1), which allows you to manage the **My Documents** window, followed by the name of the selected folder (the **My Documents** folder in this case). On the right hand end of the title bar, the **Minimize** (2) and **Maximize** (3) buttons collapse the window into its scroll bar button and enlarge the window to the full screen size, respectively, while the **Close** button (4) closes the window.
  - the **menu bar** (b): contains the different menus for managing the contents of the window.
  - the **Standard Buttons** toolbar (c): contains tool buttons to carry out certain actions quickly.
  - the left hand pane (d) contains several list boxes showing options that carry out certain actions when you click them. Five types of list boxes may appear: **File and Folder Tasks**, **Other Places**, **Picture Tasks**, **Music Tasks**, and **Details** . These boxes will offer different options according to the window item you select. If you cannot see the options that a box contains, click the ⟨⟩ button on the right of the box's title bar. Similarly, to hide a box's options, click the ⟨⟩ button, which appears in the same position.
  - the right hand pane (e) shows all the folders and files in the folder concerned (this example shows the contents of the **My Documents** folder).

*When you open a folder window, by default, Windows displays a frame containing a set of boxes and each box offers a set of options that allow you to carry out various actions. You can replace this pane by one of five explorer bars. For example, the Folders explorer bar shows your computer's folder hierarchy (the full set of folders and files that your hard disk contains) and allows you to copy, move, delete, rename or search for folders and files.*

## DISPLAYING AN EXPLORER BAR IN A FOLDER WINDOW

- Open the folder window in which you want to display an explorer bar (for example, the **My Documents** folder window, or the window of a subfolder of the **My Documents** folder).
- Click the **View** menu and point to the **Explorer Bar** option.
- Click the name of the explorer bar you want to display:
  - the **Search** bar allows you to search for folders, files, people or computers in your computing network. It also allows you to search the Internet.

- the **Favorites** bar lists all your favourite pages (whether they are on the Internet or not). You can add new page items to the list in this bar to make it easier to access these pages in the future. You can group your pages according to common themes by organizing them into different folders.
- the **Media** bar allows you to read music, video and multimedia files from the same folder window. It also provides access to the different media that the computer offers, such as Internet radio stations, for example.
- the **History** bar shows the pages (Web pages, Windows Help pages, documents and so forth) that you have visited today or in preceding days or weeks.
- the **Folders** bar displays the hierarchical structure of your computer's files, folders and devices and allows you to manage these items (by copying, moving, deleting, renaming and finding your files and folders, for example). You can also display this bar using the **start - All Programs - Accessories - Windows Explorer** command.

▨ To close an explorer bar, click the ▨ button in the top right corner of the bar.

*Although it is recommended that you work in the My Documents folder, you may still need to access folders other than those that your My Documents folder contains. For example, you may need to access another user's folders, or another drive such as a floppy-disk or a CD-ROM. For this purpose, you can use the Folders explorer bar, which displays the complete hierarchy of your hard disk.*

## ACCESSING A DRIVE OR A FOLDER

▨ Open the folder window of your choice.

▨ Display the **Folders** explorer bar either by using the **View - Explorer Bar - Folders** command or by clicking the [Folders] button on the **Standard Buttons** toolbar.

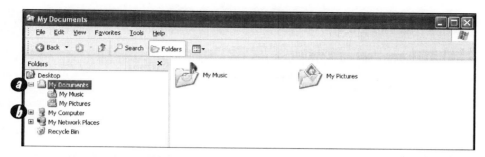

The right hand pane displays the contents of the item selected in the **Folders** bar. In this example, you see the contents of the **My Documents** folder, which is selected in the **Folders** bar.

In the example below, the **Folders** bar shows the different items of the desktop as a hierarchy: some branches of the hierarchy are expanded (a) to show the folder objects they contain, while other branches are collapsed (b). A minus sign (-) indicates an expanded branch, while a plus sign (+) indicates a collapsed branch. To expand or collapse a branch just click the + or the -. To expand a branch fully, click the folder concerned then press the * key (on the numeric keypad).

In the **Folders** bar, click **My Computer** to display the items it contains.

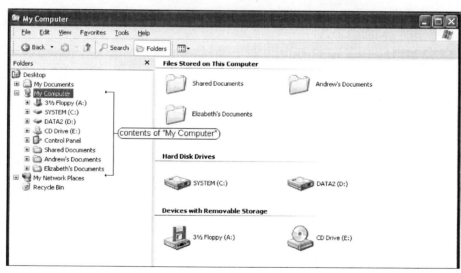

# My Documents window

The items contained in **My Computer** will vary according to the installation. However, they are generally grouped into the following categories:

- **Files Stored on This Computer** groups the folders that contain your working files.
- **Hard Disk Drives** groups your computer's hard disk drives (this example shows two hard disk drives: C: and D:).
- **Devices with Removable Storage** groups drives on your computer into which you can insert and withdraw storage units, such as floppy-disks and CD-ROMS.

Notice that different categories use different icon styles to portray their items.

▓ To view the contents of a folder or a device, click the folder or the device in the explorer bar or double-click its icon in the right-hand pane.

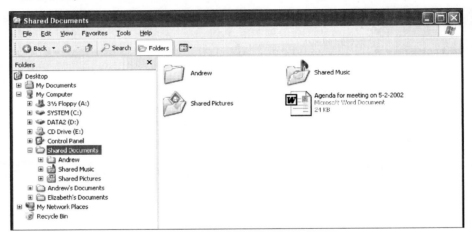

In this example, **Shared Documents** was clicked to show all the folders and files that this folder contains in the right hand pane.

To help you to distinguish a folder from a file, remember that a folder is used to store subfolders and files. A folder works in a similar way to a physical folder, which may contain dividers ("subfolders") with documents ("files") between them. A folder is always represented by this style of icon: 🗀. On the other hand, the icon for a file will vary according to the application that created it.

A folder that is not preceded by a + or - sign indicates that the folder does not contain any subfolders. However, the folder may still contain files.

When you open (expand) a folder, its icon changes (as with the **Shared Documents** folder in the example above).

▓ To access the folder on the next level up (the parent folder) you can run the **View - Go To - Up One Level** command. Alternatively, you can click the button on the **Standard Buttons** toolbar or press the backspace ⬅ key.

In the example above, clicking the tool button will display the contents of **My Computer**.

▓ To go back to the folder or device you viewed previously, you can run the **View - Go To - Back** command. Alternatively, you can click the button on the **Standard Buttons** toolbar or press the Alt ⬅ shortcut key.

▓ To go forward again to the next folder or device in the list of those you viewed, you can run the **View - Go To - Forward** command. Alternatively, you can click the button or press the Alt ➡ shortcut key.

▓ To view again one of the folders or devices you viewed since you opened the folder window, click the down-arrow on the Back or the tool button then click the name of the folder or device you want to view again.

When a folder or drive appears in the right pane, you can double-click it to view its contents.

To refresh the contents of the window so that it will take into account any changes that have occurred since you opened the window, use the **View - Refresh** command or press the F5 key.

By default, a folder window shows the name of each file along with its size, its type and a file type icon. You can change this display, for example, to view only the icon or the name of each file or to view a thumbnail (miniature) of each file.

## CHANGING THE PRESENTATION OF THE FOLDER/FILE LIST

▓ Select the folder whose presentation you want to change.

▓ Open the **View** menu or click the button.

# My Documents window

You can choose from one of six options:

**Filmstrip** available only for picture folders, this option presents each picture as a thumbnail, along with its name, in a single line. When you select a picture, a larger scale preview appears in a pane above.

**Thumbnails** presents a preview picture and the name of each file in the folder. Pictures appear as thumbnails, while other types of file appear as the logo of the application that created them.

**Tiles** shows the name of each file along with its type, size and a file type icon.

**Icons** shows only the name of each file underneath an icon representing its type.

**List** shows only the name of each file beside an icon representing its type. The files appear in the form of an ordered list in one or more columns (in alphabetical order by default). You cannot move the files to different positions in the list.

**Details** lists the files in a single column showing an icon representing the type of each file along with other information including its name, its size, its type and the date and time it was last modified.

The example below shows the contents of the **Correspondence** folder in **Details** view.

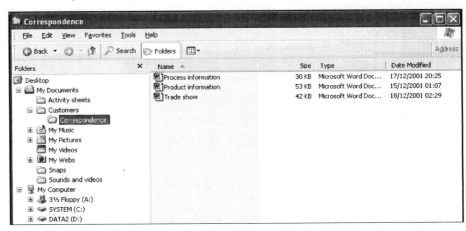

This view shows the size of each file in **kilobytes (KB)**: a byte is the space that one character occupies. The type of a file is associated with its format, which depends on the application that created the file. The icon preceding the file also depends on the application that created it, as does the filename extension (this is a set of three characters that appears as a suffix to the filename: by default, the filename extension does not appear in the folder window). The date and time of the last modification shows the system time when the file was last modified (your computer has an internal clock, which it uses for this sort of information).

- If any information in a column is not entirely visible, an ellipsis (...) appears at the end of the content (as in the **Type** column, in the above example). To view the content of a column in its entirety, you must widen the column concerned. You can do this by dragging the vertical separator line that appears to the right of the column header (for example, to the right of the **Type** header, above).

- To change the order in which the files appear in the list, use **View - Arrange Icons by** then click **Name**, **Size**, **Type** or **Modified** (date of last modification) according to how you want to sort the list.

- When your files appear in **Details** view, you can simply click the header of the column on which you want to sort. For example, clicking the **Date Modified** header will sort your files according to the date and time they were last modified. Click once to sort in ascending order; click again to sort in descending order.

# Managing folders and files

*Even if you have just bought your computer, your hard disk will not be empty: it must contain the files of the Windows XP operating system. These files are grouped together into folders. Your personal folder is present on the hard disk under the name of **My Documents**. This folder is there to accommodate the files you will create. When you have created a certain number of files, you may have trouble finding a specific document. To avoid long searches, it is recommended that you store your files in different folders that you can create for this purpose within your **My Documents** folder. Each of these folders can represent a certain theme or contain a certain type of file. For example, you could store all your files concerning your budget in a folder called **Budget**, or you could store all your letters in a folder called **Correspondence**. To draw an analogy, it is better to store your clothes on different shelves in a wardrobe, than to keep them all together in a trunk.*

## CREATING A FOLDER

▓ To create a new folder in your **My Documents** folder, open the **My Documents** folder directly. For this purpose, click the **start** button followed by the **My Documents** option.

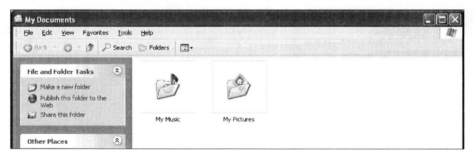

The **My Documents** window appears on the screen. Its left pane offers a number of options in the form of hyperlinks.

▓ To create a folder in your **My Documents** folder (on the same level as the **My Music** folder and the **My Pictures** folder) do not select any folder or file in the **My Documents** window.
To create a subfolder of an existing folder, double-click the folder concerned (for example, the **My Pictures** folder).

▓ Click the **Make a new folder** link in the **File and Folder Tasks** box in the left pane (if the options of this box are not visible, click the ⮛ button first). If your **File and Folder Tasks** box does not offer a **Make a new folder** link, you must have already selected a folder or file in the window. Deselect this folder or file by clicking an empty space in the right hand pane that is not occupied by any particular folder or file.

Windows Explorer

Alternatively, you can right-click an empty space of the right hand pane then choose the **New** option followed by the **Folder** option.

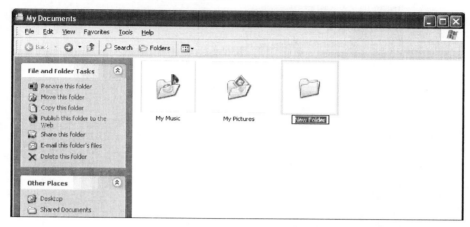

A new icon appears in the right pane. This folder is called **New Folder** for the moment: this name is highlighted and the insertion point blinks at the end of it, indicating that you can change it.

▓ Enter the name of your new folder: your name can be up to 255 characters long, including spaces. You can use uppercase or lowercase letters, or both, but you cannot insert the following characters: \ / ? : * " < > or |.

▓ Press the ⌨Enter key to validate the name of your new folder.

Windows creates your new folder, which for now is empty.

*Whatever you want to do with your folders or files (for example, to copy, move or delete one or more of them) you must start by selecting the folder(s) or file(s) concerned.*

## SELECTING FOLDERS AND FILES

▓ Open the folder window that contains the folders or files you want to select.

▓ If necessary, change the presentation of the file list using the 🔲▾ button and/or sort the file list using the **View - Arrange Icons by** command.

▓ To select several adjacent files in the list, point to an empty space just to the right of the first name you want to select then drag the mouse so that the dotted rectangle that appears surrounds the names and icons concerned then release the mouse button.

# Managing folders and files

Be careful: if the mouse pointer appears as a black circle with a diagonal bar across it and the file names move with the mouse pointer, release the mouse button immediately and start again.

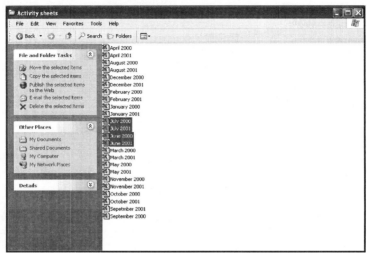

*Four files have been selected in this example.*

※ To extend your selection of adjacent files to include other files further down the list, press the **Shift** key then click the document name you would like to appear at the end of the list.

**For instance, if you want to include the March 2000 and March 2001 files in the example selection above, press the Shift key then click the March 2001 file name.**

※ To include another group of adjacent files or folders from the open folder (that is not adjacent to the existing group), press the **Shift** key then drag the mouse so that the dotted rectangle that appears surrounds the names and icons of the new group you want to include in your selection. When you are satisfied with your new selection, release the mouse button followed by the **Shift** key.

※ To include another single file or folder from the open folder (that is not adjacent to the existing group), press the **Ctrl** key then click the name of the file or folder concerned.

**For instance, if you want to include the December 2001 file into the example selection above, press the Ctrl key then click the December 2001 file name.**

Windows Explorer

- To select all the files and folders contained in the open folder, use the **Edit - Select All** command or press the ⌨Ctrl **A** key combination.
- To invert your selection, use the **Edit - Invert Selection** command.

**When you have selected a group of folders or files you can right-click your selection to view the menu options that you can apply to your selection (this is called a shortcut menu).**

**Once you have made your selection (be it a single file or a group), you can perform a variety of actions, such as deleting or copying the selected file(s).**

*To select files, you must first access the folder that contains them. If you do not know the name of the folder that contains your files, you can search for your files in all the folders on your hard disk.*

## SEARCHING FOR FILES ACCORDING TO THEIR NAMES

- Click the **start** button on the taskbar then click the **Search** option.

Alternatively, if a folder window is active, you can click the ⌕ Search tool button in this window to display the **Search Results** window.

- If necessary, click the ⊡ button in the **Search Results** window to display this window in full-screen mode and view all the options that the **Search Companion** offers.

By default, a little dog called **Rover** animates the **Search Companion** pane.

- Click the **Documents (word processing, spreadsheet, etc.)** option.

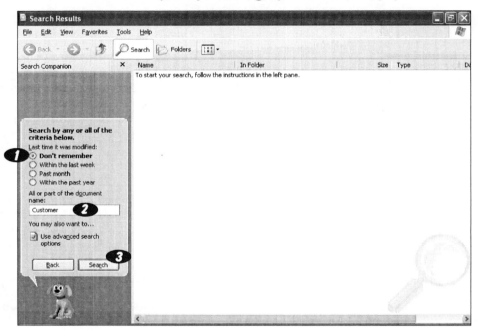

*1.* If you know when the file you seek was last modified, activate one of the three other options. Otherwise, leave the **Don't remember** option active.

*2.* Enter the name or part of the name of the document you seek. If you are not sure of the exact name of the document, you can use wildcard characters. Use the asterisk (*) to represent zero or more characters: (for example if you enter **cap\***, you will find files called **cap, cape, caption, capture** and so forth). Use the question mark (?) to represent one character (for example, if you enter **cap?**, you will find the **cape** file but not the files **cap, caption , capture** and so forth).

*3.* Click to start the search.

When Windows has finished the search, it displays the items it has found in the right hand pane.

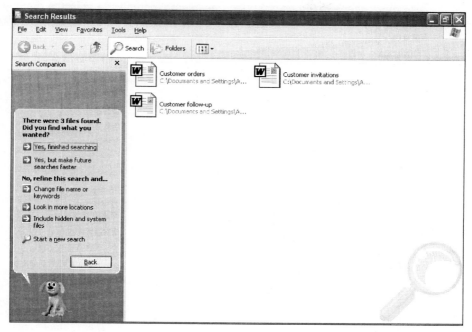

- To view a brief description of one of the files found, point to its name: a ScreenTip appears showing the file's type, author, size and so forth.

- To open one of these files, double-click its name (or its icon): the file opens along with the application that created it.

- To carry out another search, click the **Start a new search** link.

- To close the **Search Companion**, leaving the **Search Results** window open, click the **Yes, finished searching** link.

- To close the **Search Results** window, click the ⊠ button.

# Managing folders and files

When you have created your folders, you can store appropriate files or folders in them. You can always copy these files into your new folders, but this approach will use more space than necessary and needlessly complicate your file management. It is generally a much better idea simply to move your folders and files from one folder to another.

## MOVING FOLDERS AND FILES

▨ Click the **start** button then the **My Documents** option to open your personal folder window.

▨ Select the folder(s) or the file(s) you want to move.

▨ Under **File and Folder Tasks** in the left-hand pane of the window, click the **Move this folder** link or the **Move this file** link (if you selected only one folder or file) or the **Move the selected items** link (if you selected several folders and/or files).

▨ In the **Move Items** dialog box, click the name of the folder into which you want to move your folders or files. If this destination folder is not visible, click the + sign preceding the device name and the parent folder.

This example shows the **Customer orders** document being moved to the **Correspondence** subfolder of the **Shared Documents** folder.

▨ Click the **Move** button.

▨ If necessary, close the folder window.

Windows Explorer

As its name suggests, the **Make New Folder** button in the **Move Items** dialog box creates a new destination folder

*To duplicate a folder or a file, you can make a copy of it and, if you wish, rename the duplicate file.*

## COPYING FOLDERS AND FILES

▨ Click the **start** button then click the **My Documents** option to open your personal folder.

▨ In the left pane of the folder window, select the folder(s) or file(s) you want to copy.

▨ In the **File and Folder Tasks** box of the left pane, click the **Copy this file, Copy this folder** or **Copy the selected items** link, according to what you selected (if none of these options are visible, click the ⊗ button in the **File and Folder Tasks** box).

▨ In the **Copy Items** dialog box that appears, click the name of the folder into which you want to copy. If this destination folder is not visible in this dialog box, click the + sign preceding the name of the parent drive or folder.

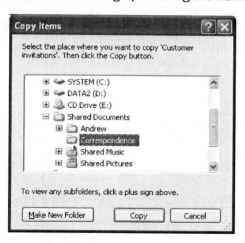

*This example shows the Customer Invitations file being copied into the Correspondence folder of the Shared Documents folder.*

▨ Click the **Copy** button.

▨ If necessary, close the folder window.

# Managing folders and files

As its name suggests, the **Make New Folder** button on the **Copy Items** dialog box can create a new destination folder.

You can also copy folders or files in a folder window, by displaying the **Folders** explorer bar and using the **Copy** and **Paste** commands in the **Edit** menu.

*You can duplicate a folder or file by copying it to a floppy disk. A floppy disk can be used to save your work, or to copy it elsewhere, or to give files to someone else.*

## COPYING FOLDERS OR FILES TO A FLOPPY DISK

▨ Check that your floppy disk drive contains a formatted floppy disk (cf. the Formatting a floppy disk section at the end of this chapter).

▨ Open the folder window that contains the folders or files you want to copy to your floppy disk.

▨ Select the folder(s) or the file(s) concerned.

▨ Use **File - Send To** then click the option corresponding to your floppy disk drive: this is often called **3½ Floppy (A)**.

A **Copying** window indicates how the copy is progressing. The noise of the floppy disk drive and its green light also indicate that the copy is underway.

A standard floppy disk cannot contain more than 1.44 MB (1.44 Megabytes) or 1474 KB (1474 Kilobytes). If the file is too big, Windows displays a message to indicate that it is unable to copy it to the floppy disk.

*To tidy up your hard disk, you can delete files you no longer need. However, deleting a file by accident can cause hours or even days of extra work. To safeguard against such handling errors, Windows deletes your files in two stages: first, Windows copies these files to the Recycle Bin. The files no longer appear in your folder, but they are still present on your disk and you can recover them at any time. To remove your files permanently from your hard disk, you must delete them from the Recycle Bin.*

## DELETING FOLDERS AND FILES

▨ Click the **start** button then the **My Documents** option to open your personal folder window.

▨ Select the folder(s) or the file(s) you want to delete.

Under **File and Folder Tasks,** click the **Delete this folder** link or the **Delete this file** link (if you selected only one folder or file) or the **Delete the selected items** link (if you selected several folders and/or files).

Alternatively, you can press the Del key or use the **File - Delete** command.

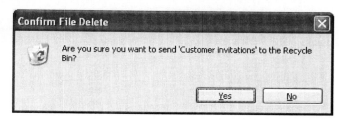

Click the **Yes** button to confirm that you want to send the folder(s) or file(s) to the Recycle Bin.

Almost immediately, the folder(s) or file(s) disappear from the folder window. **When you delete a folder, you also delete all the files and any subfolders it contains**.
This deletion is not final: the documents you have deleted are still present on the disk although they are no longer visible in your folder window.
To delete files permanently and free the disk space they occupy, you must either delete the files in the Recycle Bin or empty the Recycle Bin.
**Important note:** if you delete items from a drive other than your computer's hard disk (for example, from a floppy disk or from a drive on the network) Windows does not use the Recycle Bin and you will not be able to recover these files later.

If the files you want to delete are contained in several folders, you can run a search for them then select them in the **Search Results** window before deleting them.

To delete a file permanently from your disk without using the Recycle Bin, select it and press the Shift Del keys instead of the Del key alone. Do not use this key combination unless you are absolutely sure that you no longer need the files you have selected.

# Managing folders and files

*When you have deleted a file you can still view it in, and recover it from, a special folder called the Recycle Bin.*

## MANAGING FOLDERS AND FILES IN THE RECYCLE BIN

░ To view files you have deleted, double-click the **Recycle Bin** icon on your desktop to open this folder.

The folders and files contained in the Recycle Bin appear. You can manage this list as you would manage the list of items in any other folder: use the options of the **View** menu to define its presentation.

░ To recover one or more files or folders from the Recycle Bin, select the items concerned in this window then, under **Recycle Bin Tasks**, click the **Restore this item** link (if you selected only one folder or file) or the **Restore the selected items** link (if you selected several folders and/or files).

The files and/or folders disappear from the Recycle Bin. Windows restores each item to the folder from which it was deleted, recreating this folder if it no longer exists.

░ To restore all the items in the Recycle Bin to the folders from which they were deleted, make sure that no folder or file is selected and click the **Restore all items** link under **Recycle Bin Tasks**.

**Windows Explorer**

▧ To delete permanently one or more folders and/or files and thereby free the disk space that they occupy, select the folders and/or files in the Recycle Bin window then select **File - Delete** or press the ⌧ Del ⌧ key. Confirm your action by clicking the **Yes** button.

▧ To delete permanently all the folders and files in the Recycle Bin, click the **Empty the Recycle Bin** link under **Recycle Bin Tasks**. Confirm your action by clicking the **Yes** button.

**After you have emptied your Recycle Bin, it will remain empty until you delete other folders or files.**

To delete permanently all the folders and files in the Recycle Bin, you can also right-click the **Recycle Bin** icon on your desktop and choose the **Empty Recycle Bin** option.

*Although most commercially available floppy disks are preformatted, you may sometimes need to format or to reformat a floppy disk. This operation allows your operating system to organise the floppy disk according to the characteristics of your computer's floppy-disk drive (in particular, it determines the capacity of the floppy disk).*

## FORMATTING A FLOPPY DISK

▧ Insert the floppy disk in your floppy-disk drive.

▧ Open the **My Computer** window using the **start - My Computer** command.

▧ Right-click the icon for your floppy-disk drive, which is often called **3½ Floppy (A:)**.

▧ Click the **Format** option.

# Managing folders and files

*The capacity of the floppy disk is expressed in Megabytes (MB) or in Kilobytes (KB). Remember that a byte is the space required to store one character. The information 3.5" refers to the physical dimension of the floppy disk.*

*1.* If necessary, define the **Capacity** of the floppy disk according to its physical characteristics. For a High Density floppy disk, choose **1.44 MB**; for a Low Density floppy disk, choose **720 KB** (most modern floppy disks are High Density disks).

*2.* If required, specify the name you want to give your floppy disk. This name cannot be longer than 11 characters (for FAT file systems).

*3.* If your floppy disk has already been formatted, activate the **Quick Format** option to allow Windows to delete the contents of the floppy disk, without checking the sectors on the disk. However, if you re-format the disk often, you should regularly use the complete formatting technique to test the disk's viability.

*4.* Click the **Start** button to start formatting.

A message appears to warn you that the formatting operation will delete all the files on your floppy disk.

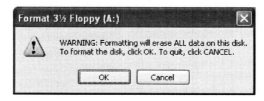

- Click the **OK** button to confirm that you want to format your floppy disk.

- At the end of the operation, click the **OK** button on the message informing you that the formatting is complete.

- Click the **Close** button in the **Format 3 1⁄2 Floppy (A:)** dialog box.

 If you try to use a floppy disk that has not been formatted, Windows will display an error message indicating that the floppy disk has not been formatted and offering to do it for you.

If Windows tells you at the end of formatting that the floppy disk contains bad (or defective) sectors, it would a good idea to throw out the floppy. Even though the system will not write data on any of the defective parts, it is a sign that the floppy is probably not reliable.

*If your computer came with a printer, you must install this device physically by connecting it to your computer via a cable, according to the manufacturer's instructions. When you run a print command, Windows sends instructions to the printer. However, each printer needs specific instructions that it can understand. For the printer to be able to understand the instructions Windows sends, your hard disk must contain a special file, called a driver. This driver provides a link between Windows and the printer. The Windows XP CD-ROM contains a large number of drivers and it probably includes one for your printer. However, if the Windows XP CD-ROM does not provide a driver for your printer, you will find one on the CD-ROM or floppy disk supplied with your printer.*

## INSTALLING A PRINTER

- Click the **start** button followed by the **Control Panel** option.

- In Category view, click the **Printers and Other Hardware** link followed by the **Add a printer** link.

  The **Add Printer Wizard** starts.

- Click the **Next** button.

# Managing folders and files

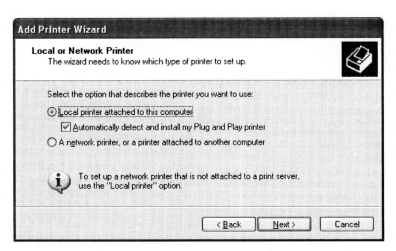

- If you have only one computer, activate the **Local printer attached to this computer** option. If you leave the **Automatically detect and install my Plug and Play printer** option active, Windows may be able to detect your newly connected printer and install it automatically.

  If your computer is part of a network and the printer is connected to another machine in the network, activate the **A network printer, or a printer attached to another computer** option.

- Click the **Next** button.

- If you are installing a network printer, leave the **Browse for a printer** option active, click the **Next** button then select one of the printers in the **Shared printers** list and click the **Next** button.

- If you are installing a local printer and the **Automatically detect and install my Plug and Play printer** option was not active in the previous screen, you can change the output port in the **Use the following port** list, if it does not correspond to the port to which you connected your printer. Click the **Next** button.

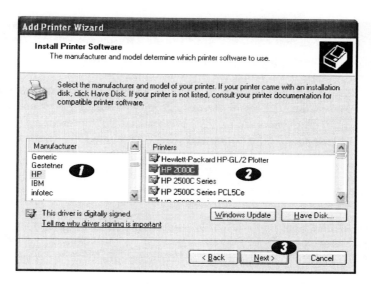

**1.** Select the make of your printer.

**2.** Select your printer model: if the exact model of your printer is not in the list, select the nearest model or insert the CD-ROM or floppy disk that contains the driver into your computer then click the **Have Disk** button. Check that the correct drive is selected in the **Copy manufacturer's files from** list then click the **OK** button and select the name of your printer.

**3.** Continue with the installation procedure.

▦ If you are installing a local printer, specify the **Printer name** in the corresponding box, if necessary.

▦ Specify whether or not Windows applications must use the printer by default then click the **Next** button.

▦ Specify whether or not you want to print a test page (printing a test page is a good idea as it allows you to check that your printer is working properly) then click the **Next** button.

▦ Click the **Finish** button.

▦ Click the ⊠ button on the **Printers and Faxes** window to close it.

# Managing folders and files

To install hardware devices on your computer such as scanners, printers or digital cameras, start the **Add Hardware Wizard**. Select **start - Control Panel - Printers and Other Hardware - Add Hardware** link (in the **See Also** box) then follow the installation procedure.

It is much simpler to install a USB device: just connect the device to one of the USB ports of your computer (you do not even need to switch your computer off to do this) and the installation procedure runs automatically. Follow the installation steps.

*After you have bought a software application on a CD-ROM or a floppy disk, you must install it on your hard disk before you can use it (installing an application consists of copying the application files onto your hard disk and defining settings to make the application work). You would generally carry out this operation using an installation wizard, which asks you certain questions as the installation progresses (such as on which drive you want to install your application and whether you want to install the full version or a limited one).*

## INSTALLING A PROGRAM (APPLICATION)

You need to use a Computer administrator type of account to install some programs.

▓ If your application is on a CD-ROM, insert the CD-ROM in your computer's CD-ROM drive.

Most applications on CD-ROM offer an Autorun or setup feature, which installs the application automatically.

▓ In this case, click the **Install** button to start the installation process and follow the instructions that appear on the screen (these instructions vary from one application to another).

▓ If your application does not install itself automatically (or if your application is on a floppy disk) access the **Control Panel** (**start - Control Panel**) then (in Category view) click the **Add or Remove Programs** link.

Windows Explorer

A list of the applications currently installed on your hard disk appears in this dialog box:

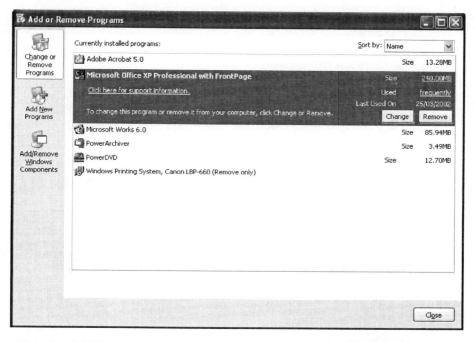

Click the **Add New Programs** button followed by the **CD or Floppy** button.

Insert the application's CD-ROM or first floppy disk in the appropriate drive of your computer, as Windows asks you to, then click the **Next** button.

Windows searches your CD-ROM or floppy disk for the application's installation program then displays its name in the **Open** box. You can use the **Browse** button to look for your installation program manually.

Click the **Finish** button to start the installation procedure.

Windows copies the files it needs to install the application.

Follow the different steps of the installation program, until the end.

When you have installed an application, its name appears in the **start - All Programs** menu, which is common to all the users of the computer. You can run your application from this menu.

# Managing folders and files

*When you no longer need an application it is a good idea to uninstall it. Rather than simply deleting the folder that contains the application's files, you are strongly advised to follow the uninstall procedure set out below.*

## UNINSTALLING A PROGRAM (APPLICATION)

Before you attempt to uninstall a program, you may need to logon with a Computer administrator type account.

- Access the **Control Panel** from the **start** menu.
- Click the **Add or Remove Programs** link (in Category view).
- Click the **Change or Remove Programs** button in the left of the window.
- In the **Currently installed programs** list, click the row corresponding to the program you want to remove.

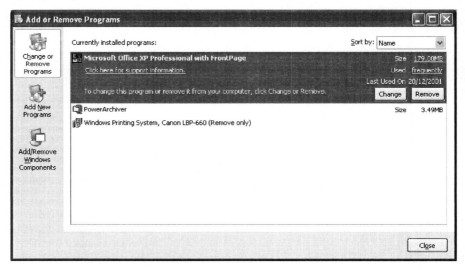

According to the application concerned, Windows may provide a **Change** button and a **Remove** button or a single **Change/Remove** button.

- Click the **Remove** button or the **Change/Remove** button.

**Windows Explorer**

Windows asks you to confirm your action.

- Click the **Yes** button.

  Windows removes all the application files you no longer need.

- When Windows has finished the uninstall procedure, click the **OK** button.

- Click the **Close** button in the **Add or Remove Programs** dialog box.

- Click the  button to close the **Control Panel**.

*Windows XP offers several multimedia applications, such as the Windows Media Player, which you can use for playing audio CDs, watching DVDs and so on. Internet technology plays such an important role in our daily lives; you can use your computer to discover a new world of information, via the "global village".*

# 5<sup>th</sup> Part

# Multimedia and communication

# Windows Media Player

*The Microsoft Windows Media Player can read a large number of audio and video file formats from your computer or from the Internet. You can use the Windows Media Player to listen to radio stations from anywhere in the world, read and copy CDs, read DVDs (if you have a DVD drive) or look for available videos on the Internet. It will even manage customized lists of all the digital multimedia files stored on your computer.*

## DISCOVERING THE WINDOWS MEDIA PLAYER

▓ To open this application, click the **start** button then **All Programs - Windows Media Player**.

these two buttons close the window

click to hide or display the taskbar

▓ The **Windows Media Player** window contains:
- a title bar and menus (a): this area appears automatically when you point to the **Playlist Selection** area (b). To keep this bar on the screen or make it disappear again, click the ⬙ button on the **Playlist Selection** area.
- the player display area (c).
- the **Playlist Selection** area (d): you can use the buttons in this area to choose a playlist or another type of element or to display play and playlist tools.

- the **Features Taskbar** (e): this bar contains seven or eight buttons; each button runs a specific feature (you can also access these features using the **View - Taskbar** menu option).
- the **Playback Controls** (f) area.

If your Internet connection is open when you start the **Windows Media Player**, it will display the contents of the WindowsMedia.com site in its monitor automatically. If you have an on-demand connection (via a modem for example) click the **Media Guide** button then confirm your request to access the network to obtain the guide's contents. If you do not request a connection, the reader display area stays black.

Select **View - Skin Mode** or ⎡Ctrl⎤ **2** or [image] to give your **Media Player** a skin appearance and select **View - Full Mode** or ⎡Ctrl⎤ **1** or double-click [image] to restore your **Media Player** to its normal appearance.

*When you play an audio CD, Windows Media Player provides an attractive interface, including an effect called a visualization, whose look you can alter to suit your taste.*

## PLAYING AN AUDIO CD

If it is closed, open the **Windows Media Player** application (**start - All Programs - Windows Media Player**) then insert an audio CD in your CD-ROM drive.

If you insert an audio CD before starting the **Windows Media Player** application, Windows XP may show you this window:

# Windows Media Player

※ If this happens, click the **Play Audio CD using Windows Media Player** option and click **OK**; this will activate the Windows Media Player and start playing the CD.

track now playing

playlist pane

If the Windows Media Player does not recognize your CD, it will show "Artist Unknown".

※ If necessary, click the **Now Playing** button on the **Features Taskbar**.

※ In the **Playlist** pane, click the required track then click the ⊙ button on the **Playback Controls** area to start playing the track (once you activate it, this button changes into ⊙).

※ Once it starts playing, use these commands to manage the playback options:

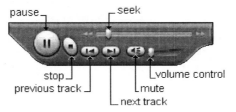

pause — seek

stop — volume control
previous track — mute
next track

The track currently playing appears in green in the **Playlist** pane and the length already played is shown at the bottom right of the window.

▓ To change the visualization that appears in the centre of the player in the **Now Playing** page, use the **View - Visualizations** command on the menu bar then activate the required view.

You can also click the  button at the bottom left of the player and choose one of the options offered. There are not as many options here as in the **Visualizations** menu.

*You can listen to some national and international radio stations over the Internet: a continuous broadcasting process makes this possible. For the user, the main advantage of this is that he or she can listen to the radio without waiting for sound files to be loaded, avoiding a "chopped" sound effect. To carry out the following actions, your Internet connection must be open.*

## LISTENING TO THE RADIO

### Looking at the Radio Tuner

▓ If it is closed, open the **Windows Media Player** application (**start - All Programs - Windows Media Player**).

▓ Click the **Radio Tuner** button on the **Features Taskbar**.

By default, the Windows Media Player displays the radio information available on the WindowsMedia.com Web site:

The Player window shows links to radio stations, classified into three categories: **Featured Stations**, **My Stations** and **Recently Played Stations**.

# Windows Media Player

- To show or hide the contents on any of these categories, click the corresponding  button.

### Finding a radio station

- Click the **Radio Tuner** button on the **Features Taskbar**.
- To make a station search, click one of the required radio types located in the right pane of the screen, or enter in the appropriate text box a keyword representing the station you want to find. If you enter a keyword, finish by clicking the ⇨ button.

  **WindowsMedia.com lists the stations that correspond to your search and also allows you to qualify your search request with more criteria:**

‹ Return to My Stations
Browse by Genre:
World Music
Search:
Search Keyword
Zip Code (US Only):
Zip Code
Use Advanced Search

- To make a combined search using a genre and a keyword, fill in the **Browse by Genre** box and the **Search** box then click the ⇨ button to the right of the **Search** box, to start the search.

  **The Zip Code search criterion is valid only in the USA.**

- To return to the previous page, click the **Return to My Stations** link.

### Listening to a radio station

- Click the **RadioTuner** button on the **Features Taskbar**.
- If the radio station to which you want to listen is not in any of the three categories offered, make a search to view it (cf. Finding a radio station, above).
- Click the link corresponding to the radio station concerned, to see some details about it.

* Click the ▶ **Play** button to listen to the selected station.

You can also listen to a station by clicking the [▷] button just to the left of its name.

Note that each time you start listening to a radio station, your PC's Web browser (such as Internet Explorer) opens and displays the active station's home page: additional advertising screens, called pop-ups may also appear. You can quickly get swamped by these! If you wish to see or close a pop-up, you may first have to activate it by clicking its button on the taskbar.

* To stop the radio, click the [●] button in the **Playback Controls** area.

## MEDIA PLAYER AND DVDS

### Playing a DVD

* Insert the DVD in the DVD drive.

# Windows Media Player

Windows Media Player may start automatically. However, if your computer has several DVD playing applications and the Media Player window is not open, the following dialog box appears so that you can choose the application you want to use:

░ Click the **Play DVD Video using Windows Media Player** option.

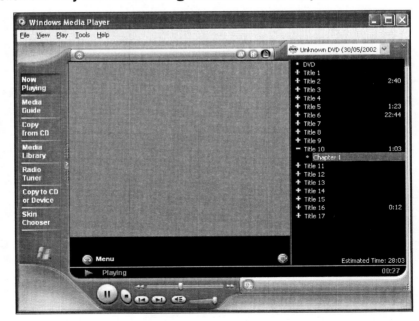

The contents of the DVD appear in the Playlist pane. In the example above, the DVD contains 17 titles and each title contains one or more chapters.

- To view the chapters for a title, click the + sign to the left of the title concerned. To hide the chapters for a title, click the - sign to the left of the title concerned.

- To play a DVD manually, open the **Play** menu and use the **DVD or CD Audio** command, or open the ⊞ My playlist ▾ list and click the name of the DVD you want to play.

- In the Playlist pane, click the title or chapter of the DVD you want to play.

- To view your DVD in full screen mode, select the **View - Full Screen** command or press [Alt][Enter] or click the button.

  When you switch to full screen view, the Player controls appear briefly then disappear.

click to activate the Windows Media Player ¬
hide or mask the playlist panel ¬

These items disappear automatically from the screen after a few moments.

- To restore these controls to the screen, move your mouse or press any key.

Before you start playing a DVD, it is advisable to deactivate the screen saver. Select the **Tools - Options - Player** tab then deactivate the **Allow screen saver during playback** option.
To specify any **Parental control** or **Language settings**, select **Tools - Options - DVD** tab and choose the required options.

## Capturing a still picture from a DVD

- Play the DVD concerned.

- **View - DVD Features - Image Capture**

  The **Image Capture** command will be available only if your graphics card and your DVD decoder support this feature.

# Windows Media Player

- If necessary, select the folder in which you want to save the image then enter the **File name**.
- If necessary, change the **Save as type** option.
- Click the **Save** button.

*You can change the look of your Windows Media Player by applying different "skins" (or presentations) to it.*

## CHANGING THE LOOK OF THE WINDOWS MEDIA PLAYER

- If it is closed, open the **Windows Media Player** application (**start** - **All Programs** - **Windows Media Player**).
- Click the **Skin Chooser** button on the **Features Taskbar**.

***1.*** Click one of the skins offered: a preview of your selected skin appears in the right part of the window.

***2.*** To apply the selected skin to the Windows Media Player, click the **Apply Skin** button.

The Windows Media Player takes on the selected appearance. This is always divided into two sections:

- To return to **Full Mode** view, double-click the  symbol or press ⌈Ctrl⌉ **1**.

- To adopt the **Skin Mode** again, click the ▓ button or choose the **Skin Mode** option in the **View** menu or press ⌈Ctrl⌉ **2**.

To download other skins from the WindowsMedia.com site, click the **More Skins** button (your Internet connection must be open) then download one of the skins on offer by clicking the appropriate link.

# Getting started on the Internet

*Although the Internet is made up of complicated technologies, you do not need to understand them before you can use it. Below you will find all the information you need to get started.*

## ACCESSING THE INTERNET

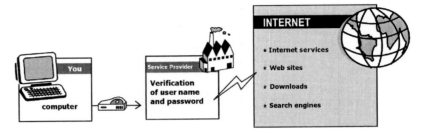

This diagram illustrates the principle of Internet access for home users.

- To access the Internet, you will need a contract with a service provider. You will also need a modem for your computer, which will communicate with the service provider, or, more precisely, with the service provider's computer.

- The service provider's computer will ask for your username, or login, and your password. If these are correct, you will then be able to use the Internet.

- Here is what you need to connect to the Internet:
  - a connection method and an appropriate modem for this method,
  - a contract with an Internet Service Provider (ISP),
  - a computer with a modem that has been configured to know which ISP it must contact.

*When you have looked at all the different connection options and chosen your ISP, you will be ready to install everything you need to connect.*

## THE DIFFERENT STEPS TO CONNECTION

### 1 - Installing your modem

- If the modem is not already installed, you will need to install it. Refer to the instructions for physically installing the modem then to those for installing the necessary driver (this is a file that will enable the modem to communicate with your computer's operating system).

Multimedia and communication

- Before you start to install your connection kit, it is a good idea to check that your modem is correctly installed:
  - Click **start - Control Panel - Printers and Other Hardware - Phone and Modem Options - Modems** tab.
  - If you can see your modem in the modem list with the correct name then your modem is installed correctly.
- If there is a problem, refer to the manual you received with the modem to find the correct configuration, or contact the hardware supplier. Your ISP helpline will probably be able to resolve minor problems.

## 2 - Contacting your chosen ISP

- First, contact the ISP to subscribe to the service.
- Your ISP will supply the information you will need to connect to the Internet:
  - your username or login,
  - your password,
  - your e-mail address.

Your ISP will also supply more technical information such as:

  - the name of the POP server,
  - the name of the SMTP server,
  - the name of the news server,
  - the telephone number for the ISP's server.
- You should also receive a connection kit (a CD-ROM) including a program that will install your connection and the necessary software automatically.

 **Some connection kits allow you to subscribe to an ISP, without having first contacted the provider.**

### 3 - Installing the connection kit

※ The CD-ROM should run automatically, but if it does not, follow the instructions it provides.

※ The program provided by your ISP will install a number of applications automatically:

- a browser (Internet Explorer or Netscape Navigator),
- an e-mail and news program (such as Outlook Express or Netscape Messenger).

**If any of these applications is already present on your computer, you can still install the ISP's programs. If the version you have is older than that of the ISP, it will be updated or if you have the same version, the ISP's application will replace it.**

※ The program will configure these applications (by defining settings such as the names of the POP and SMTP servers) and configure your Internet connection. You will need to give some information, such as:

- your username,
- your password,
- your e-mail address.

※ If you have chosen AOL as your ISP, the applications provided will be specific to AOL. If you have any questions, you will need to call the AOL helpline.

 **If you are using only one ISP, your computer will connect to this provider automatically when you launch your browser. However, you can choose to install several connections if you want to use more than one ISP to access the Internet.**

*Internet, the Web, e-mail, discussion groups... what does it all mean?*

## UNDERSTANDING THE DIFFERENT USES OF THE INTERNET

- The term Internet simply describes the network (the wires, basically) that enables you to access the services.
- The most frequently used services are:
  - e-mail,
  - searches for information,
  - file transfers (downloading software, images, videos, music and so on),
  - themed discussion groups.
- Other services include online chat, telephony and webcams.

  These services all use the Internet network, but are independent of each other. You can access each of them via a specific protocol and a specific application.

# Working with the browser

*Along with e-mail, the Web is the most popular service that the Internet offers, so much so that the two terms are commonly confused. However, the Web is in fact only a part of the Internet. You can access it via a browser.*

## UNDERSTANDING THE WEB AND THE ROLE OF BROWSERS

- The Web, or World Wide Web, is a collection of over a billion pages that contain mostly text, images, graphics and photos. It is growing all the time. These Web pages are generally contained on sites, maintained by companies, organisations or domains.

- Your browser lets you see the content of these pages. When you installed your Internet connection, your browser was configured either automatically or manually.

- The most popular browsers are Internet Explorer and Netscape Navigator. The former is installed automatically on your PC with Windows XP (or Windows 2000); it is also installed on the Mac. The latter is included in the Netscape Communicator suite. Both are freely available for download from the Microsoft site (http://www.microsoft.com) or the Netscape site (http://www.netscape.com).

*To access a Web site you must first start your browser so that it appears on the screen.*

## STARTING YOUR BROWSER

- Click the **start** button on the task bar at the bottom of the Windows desktop then drag the mouse pointer to the **Internet** option and click.

  **The application (your browser software) appears in a window. If you are not already connected to the Internet, the dial-up connection process will start automatically. Let the modem call your ISP, who will verify your username and password.**

Multimedia and communication

146

*The Microsoft Internet Explorer 6 window.*

**What you see on your screen may not correspond exactly to what is shown in these illustrations. Nevertheless, it is important to pick out the basic tools in your browser.**

**a.** The menu bar.

**b.** This icon might be that of Netscape, Internet Explorer, or your ISP.

**c.** The address bar.

**d.** The Web page display.

*Below you can learn how to use these essential tools. They were created in Illinois in 1993 by the creators of Mosaic, the first browser, and are so efficient that all current browsers use them. This means that if you change from one browser to another, you will never be completely lost.*

## DISPLAYING YOUR FIRST WEB PAGE

▦ Click in the text box on the address bar (c).

▦ Delete the text that is there and replace it with the address of the site you want to visit. For example, type **http://www.eni-publishing.com**.

# Working with the browser

When you type a Web address, remember:
- not to use apostrophes,
- not to use spaces,
- that the only characters allowed (apart from letters and numbers) are the forward slash (/), hyphens (-), underscores (_) and full stops (.).

▦ Confirm by pressing Enter.

The (b) icon begins to turn and the status bar indicates how close the page is to loading.

▦ When the icon stops turning and the status bar reads **Done** or **Document: Done**, the page you wanted is fully displayed in the window (d) (if you typed the address of a site, the site's homepage is shown).

If you cannot see all of the page contents, use the scroll bars to the right and at the bottom of the window to discover the entire page.
If the page takes too long to display and you lose patience, click the

**Stop** button ▣ to stop the page from loading, then try another address.

*The Web uses a hyperlink system, in which you go from one page to another by clicking hyperlinks. In each page you will find one or more links. When you activate a link, it starts loading another page, in which you will find yet more hyperlinks.*

## ACTIVATING HYPERLINKS IN A PAGE

▦ To find where the links are in a page, move the mouse pointer around. When the pointer takes the shape of a hand, it is over a link.

*A link might take the form of certain words in the text or of an image.*
*When you point to a link, the address of the page to which it leads appears*
*on the status bar at the bottom of the window.*

▓ Traditionally, text that is associated with a link appears in blue and is underlined, but fewer and fewer web pages respect this convention as designers place more importance on the aspect of their pages. The best way to find links is to move the mouse pointer all around the page, not forgetting to use the scroll bars, of course!

▓ To activate a link and display a new page, click the link in question.

▓ Some links go from page to page within the same site, in which case the beginning of the address (the site or server's address) stays the same:

▓ Other links will send you to a different site and you will notice a change in the appearance of the pages and a different address in the browser's address bar.

**Happy surfing!**

# E-mail

*Along with the Web browser, e-mail is one of the most popular services that the Internet provides. You can send your e-mail messages to other people who have an Internet connection, in only a few moments. When you send a message it first goes to a computer called an outgoing mail server, which reads your recipient's address and sends it on in the right direction. Conversely, when you receive a message, your incoming mail server stores it for you. Your ISP manages these servers and provides your mailbox at your e-mail address (do not confuse e-mail addresses with Web page addresses).*

## E-MAIL ADDRESSES

▨ You can recognise e-mail addresses because they contain the @ character.

▨ An e-mail address takes this form: user_name@server_name.

| | |
|---|---|
| **user_name** | this is the name or assumed name of the address' owner. It is often created using the first name (or initial) and surname of the person, which are sometimes separated with a hyphen or full stop. For example:<br>anne.watson@server_name<br>awatson@server_name<br>However, there are many variants! |
| **@** | a special character known as **at**. |
| **server_name** | this identifies the computer that stores the mailbox. |

▨ The server's name will depend on what sort of e-mail you have:

- Mailbox with your ISP:
  anne.watson@serviceprovider.co.uk

- Mailbox at your workplace:
  anne.watson@company.co.uk

- Web-based mailbox (e-mail that you access by logging on to a Web site, offered by several sites such as Yahoo!, Hotmail.com, Lycos.co.uk):
  annewatson@yahoo.co.uk

**This last type of e-mail is convenient if you are often on the move, because you can use it to check your e-mail from any computer.**

*All e-mail applications provide the same basic features. Only if you are using a Web-based mailbox will you have to get used to something a little different.*

## GETTING TO KNOW YOUR E-MAIL SOFTWARE

▓ First find the following in your program (or Web-based mailbox):

    **a.** Inbox.

    **b.** Messages you have sent.

    **c.** Messages that are ready to be sent.

    **d.** Draft messages.

    **e.** Waste bin (or trash).

▓ In **Outlook Express**:

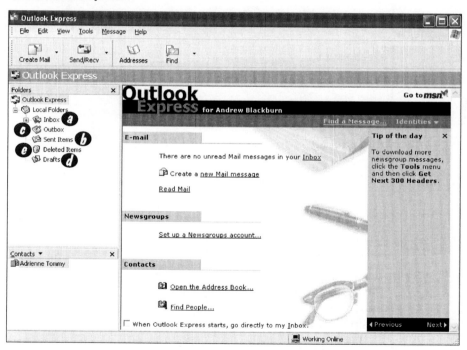

# E-mail

*The techniques detailed in this section are based on the Outlook Express e-mail program. Nevertheless, you should not have any trouble finding the equivalent commands in other e-mail software and Web-based e-mail.*

## SENDING A MESSAGE

Before you can do this, your e-mail program needs to be correctly configured, which means that it needs to know the names of your incoming and outgoing mail servers, your e-mail address, and your name.

▨ Open your e-mail program.

▨ **Message - New Message** or `Create Mail` or `Ctrl` **N**

A **New Message** window appears.

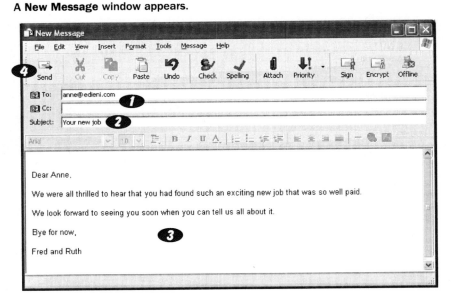

1.  Type the recipient's address carefully: unlike postmen, computers can deliver messages only if the address has been typed correctly. If you are sending the message to several people, separate the addresses with semi-colons.

2.  Type in a few words to give the message a subject. This should resume the message contents and is important, because many people manage their incoming messages according to the subject.

3.  Enter the text of the message here. You can write as much as you like.

Multimedia and communication

**4.** Click this button to send the message.

**Once the message has been sent, it appears in the sent messages box.**

It is a good idea to prepare all your messages offline. You should connect to the Internet only to send and receive messages, as this will keep your connection times short.

*As this chapter described previously, you will need to ask your server to send your new e-mail messages to your computer before you can read them.*

## COLLECTING YOUR MAIL

▓ Click the  button.

**This command will copy your messages onto your hard drive. You can disconnect as soon as you have finished.**

▓ Now open the new mail folder: the **Inbox**.

# E-mail

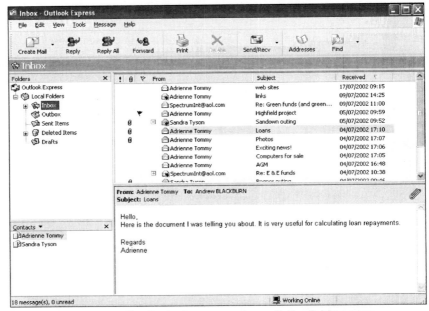

*You can see the **Contacts** pane underneath the **Folders** pane.*

▒ Double-click a message to read its contents.

**The message appears in a new window.**

*In addition to text, you can attach documents to your messages (such as pictures, graphs and spreadsheets). For example, imagine that you are planning a family party and you want to send your menu ideas to your sister, who lives at the other end of the country. You can type out your ideas in Word (for example), then send them to your sister, who can make any changes she might think appropriate. Once she has made her changes, she can return the Word file to you by e-mail, along with a list of all the guests in an Excel file. These documents are sent as attachments to the e-mails.*

## ATTACHED FILES (ATTACHMENTS)

▒ Write the message as described above.

▒ Use the **Insert - File Attachment** command in Outlook Express.

▒ Select the file you want to attach to the message then click **Open** or **Attach**.

▒ Repeat these steps if you want to attach more files.

▓ Now send the message.

When you receive an attached file, a paper clip appears next to the message. Open the message and double-click the attachment icon. The e-mail application then asks you if you want to open or to save the file. Be careful here, as attachments often carry viruses (a virus is a program that destroys or damages files on your disk). Installing an anti-virus program on your computer is an excellent idea, but may not be enough: new viruses appear every day. For effective protection you must update your anti-virus program regularly, either automatically using a subscription or manually from the Internet.

However, you can limit considerably the risk of catching a virus, simply by not opening e-mails you receive from unknown sources.

# 6th Part

You have no doubt realised that Windows has to work hard to juggle between the system, all the open applications and the (sometimes dubious!) actions that we carry out. It is little wonder that sometimes things go wrong! This last section shows you some of the more common error messages that you may see and the various problems that can occur, with a few troubleshooting tips.

# Troubleshooting

## 6.1 Technical problems

p.158

# Technical problems

*When you start Windows, it begins by scrolling comments on black screens before showing the desktop. Sometimes, however, unexpected problems may occur.*

## FLOPPY DISK

▒ You may see the following message:

**Non-system disk or disk error**

**Replace and strike any key when ready**

▒ When Windows starts up, it tries to read specific files that contain information on the hardware and its general configuration. This message indicates that your computer was unable to find these files.

- In most cases, this message means that there is a disk in the floppy disk drive. If you remove this floppy disk then press any key, Windows should be able to start normally.

- If this is not the case, these files have probably been deleted, damaged or moved: consult your computer dealer or a person who has in-depth knowledge of your operating system.

*You want to access a drive (such as a floppy, zip or CD-ROM drive) but Windows will not let you do so.*

## DRIVE INACCESSIBLE

▒ Windows shows a message telling you that it cannot read this drive:

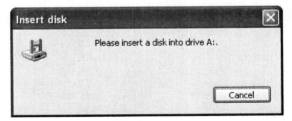

▒ Check that you selected the right drive and that your drive contains a storage device (such as a floppy disk, a ZIP disk or a CD-ROM).

*While you are working on your computer, a blue screen suddenly appears telling you that a system error has occurred.*

## SYSTEM ERROR

▧ This message usually starts with the letters OE followed by other letters and numbers: these are memory addresses. It means that different items are occupying the same place in memory (this is called a memory conflict). To solve this problem, Windows invites you to press the keys [Ctrl] [Alt] and [Del] simultaneously. This action allows the system to restart (or to reboot).

If you made any changes to open documents without saving them to disk before this incident occurred, you will lose these changes.

*When you start an application or while you are working with it, you may see a message referring to a specific file.*

## FILE ERRORS

▧ If the message indicates an error in a file (in a .DLL file, for example), try stopping and restarting the application.

If the message indicates that Windows could not find a file that it needs to carry out an action you requested, try again. If the message appears once more, you may need to re-install the application. To ensure that you do not aggravate the problem, contact your computer store or computer hotline.

*While you are working on your computer, Windows may show a warning window after it was unable to find a file it needed.*

## CLOSE WINDOW

▧ In most cases you need only click the **Close** button: Windows will shut down the application, which you can then restart.

In computing jargon, people speak of a system having "crashed". This means that for some (hardware or software) technical reason, the system is unable to carry out your request. There are generally not many things you can do in this case. If your computer is completely blocked, restart it. If you suspect your hardware to be the root of the problem, check your connections. Otherwise, restart your computer and your application. Very often, everything will then be alright: you may have lost only the latest changes you made to the document on which you were working at the time of the crash (the changes you made since you last saved your document to disk).

# Technical problems

If your computer does not switch off immediately when you press the Power button, keep this button pressed in for a few seconds.

*With certain Windows applications, such as Word, you may find that when you choose a certain option, the application will show a message to tell you that it needs a certain component in order to comply with your request.*

## OFFICE APPLICATION MESSAGE

▓ A dialog box appears offering to install a new feature.

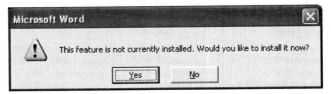

As the section on **Managing folders and files** describes, applications are often installed with only those features that are most commonly used. With this message, the application indicates that it needs a feature that is not currently installed and offers to install it for you.

▓ If you want to go ahead with your action, insert the Office suite CD-ROM in your CD-ROM drive and click **Yes** or **OK**.

Windows will get the missing file(s) from the CD-ROM then you can carry on working.

▓ If you do not want to install this feature, click **No** or **Cancel**.

Windows will then allow you to carry on working without using this feature.

*And when the hardware gets involved...*

## HARDWARE PROBLEM

▧ A common cause of hardware problems is the cable connection.

▧ When you start up your computer, you may find that a <u>hardware item is no longer working</u> (such as your mouse, for example) even though it was working correctly the last time you used your computer. First, check all the connections: for example, you could take out and put back in each connection in turn. This simple approach alone may be enough to solve the problem.

▧ If your <u>main unit does not start</u>: are you sure it is switched on? Some central units have an on/off switch on the back panel with the connectors: is this switch in the | or **on** position? If so, check that the unit's **on** indicator is lit: if it is not lit then you may have a real problem and you must contact the computer store that supplied you with the machine.

▧ The <u>number pad does not work</u>: have you activated the Num Lock? Check the [Num Lock] indicator just above the number pad: if it is not lit, press the [Num Lock] key to activate the Num Lock and light this indicator.

*Suppose that you must print some important documents, but your printer is leaving traces on the paper.*

## PRINTER PROBLEM

▧ If you have a laser printer, clean the corona wire on the drum. Consult your printer's user manual for this purpose. With some models, when you take out the drum you can see a mirror: it is sometimes sufficient simply to clean this mirror (above all, do not use any cleaning products for this purpose: use only a soft dry cloth).

▧ Ink jet printers may also leave traces. This problem is usually caused by dirty ink cartridges: you should be able to solve this problem by removing the ink cartridges and cleaning them.

*Unexpected pages may appear when you are surfing the Web.*

## INTERNET ERRORS

▧ Two types of Internet error messages most frequently occur:

**Error 404**     indicates that a page of an existing site is not available. Click the **Back** button in your browser and test another link.

# Technical problems

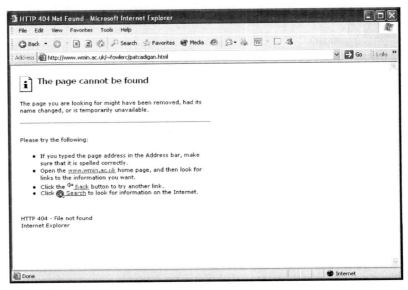

**Cannot display page** indicates that an Internet site or page is not available. Try clicking the **Back** button in your browser and repeating your action.

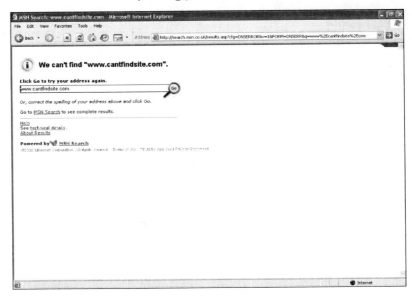

# —Index

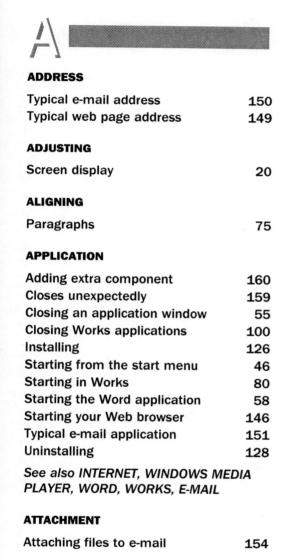

# —Index—

# —Index——————————

# —Index

# —Index

# —Index

# —Index

## S

# —Index

# —Index—

# —Index

## Z

**ZIP**